MULTIMEDIA BUILDING TECHNIQUES FOR
SCALE MODEL AIRCRAFT

MULTIMEDIA BUILDING TECHNIQUES FOR SCALE MODEL AIRCRAFT

Robin Carpenter

THE CROWOOD PRESS

First published in 2020 by
The Crowood Press Ltd
Ramsbury, Marlborough
Wiltshire SN8 2HR

enquiries@crowood.com

www.crowood.com

British Library Cataloguing-in-Publication Data
A catalogue record for this book is available from the British Library.

ISBN 978 1 78500 723 1

Typeset and designed by D & N Publishing, Baydon, Wiltshire

Printed and bound in India by Replika Press Pvt Ltd

Contents

Introduction

Like many modellers I have met over the years, from an early age I have been building plastic model kits. Birthdays and Christmases would be filled with the anticipation of looking at the latest Airfix kit release. As I grew older, my enthusiasm for building kits didn't stop, even during my years of service in the Royal Navy. Having this hobby as a lifelong companion has allowed me to see clearly how things have changed: from the early days of a 1/72-scale cockpit represented with a single bar the pilot sat on, to today's kits that have a complete cockpit interior.

This book is an introduction and guide to adding those extra details, using multimedia accessories to add finesse to a standard plastic scale model aircraft. There is only a certain amount of detail that injection-moulded plastic can achieve, but by using slide moulding, manufacturers are getting better detail definition all the time. Some manufacturers now include extras such as etched brass to their kits, giving the option to use either the plastic parts or the etched brass parts. There are also multimedia kits available that will typically include etched brass, polyurethane resin, white metal and

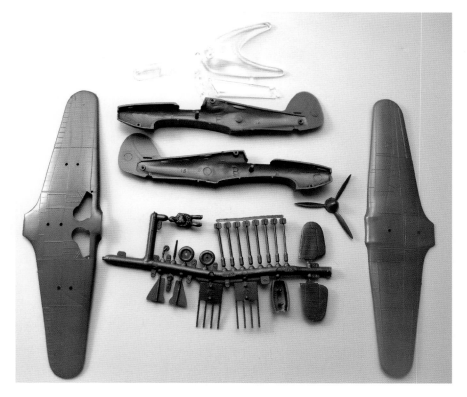

An early 1/72-scale Hawker Hurricane from Airfix, with very few parts. The pilot is seated on the protruding peg, and no other cockpit details or options are included.

even wood, and there is a plethora of manufacturers of etched brass and resin accessories.

The modeller now has plenty of choice to enhance areas of his model for a more accurate representation of the aircraft he is building, although with some older kits additional parts may not be available, so some scratch building or cross kitting will be required. With what is currently available in the market place, modellers can make a minor adjustment – for example, by just changing the wheels – or they can go the whole hog, getting everything available for the chosen aircraft to build a super detailed model.

Building model aircraft using the extra detail sets available can be very satisfying, but it is worth giving some thought to how much of the detail will be visible once the model is fully built. Much will be dependent on the kit scale, of course, as generally, the larger the scale the more detail can be seen. It is entirely up to the builder as to how much is done, and eyesight and patience play their part. For some modellers, knowing that the inside of the rear fuselage is as detailed as the real thing will give a great deal of satisfaction, even though only a small amount of it can be seen.

In the preparation of this book I would like to thank Alex Medwell and all the staff from The Airbrush Company for their unfailing support with supply, facilitation and support of my model finishing courses; also Ann McCarten and staff at Precision Photofabrication Developers Ltd (PPD Ltd) for access to, and photography of their production line; Mr Tim Perry for access to 3D printing processes; and my wife Rosemary, who has supported me in my hobby and helped me put this book together.

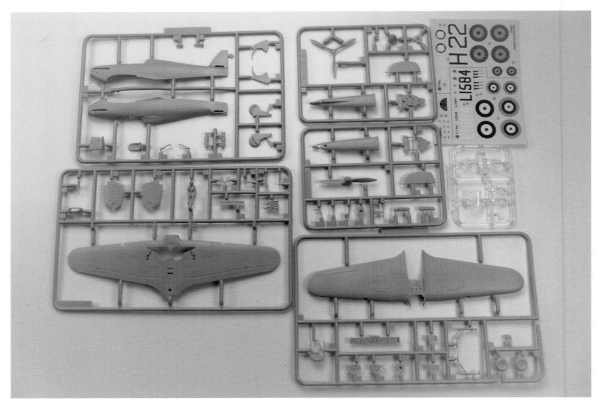

Compare this with the previous picture: this is the latest 1/72-scale Hawker Hurricane from Airfix, with options to replicate either an early or a late Mark 1 Hurricane, including two options of an early or a late fully detailed cockpit.

Chapter One

Basic Plastic Kit-Building Techniques

Even if you were making models in childhood or adolescence, it is possible there are new techniques and materials that have developed recently, with which you are not familiar. There are many kits that now come with etched brass, resin and white metal included, which must be used to complete the kit, and many plastic kits, even expensive ones, can turn up problems, such as short shot sprues or warpages. This chapter is written both as an introduction and as a refresher for some of these techniques.

TOOLS

Tools are an important part of a modeller's arsenal. It is very easy to accumulate tools, but before you buy another, it is worth thinking about how much modelling you do, and whether you are really going to use it. Every modeller will have a budget, and there are tools available to suit every pocket. However, a successful ethos when buying tools is to get the best quality you can afford, as cheap tools rarely last well. A basic tool kit for building a standard plastic kit should consist of the following:

- Craft knives with a selection of different-shaped blades
- Razor saws, both fine and coarse cut
- Sprue/side cutters
- Tweezers, with both fine points and flat ends

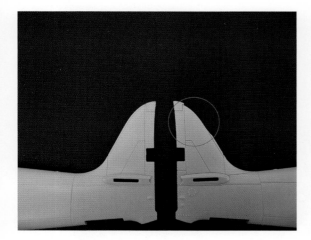

A short shot fuselage where the plastic did not fill the mould correctly. This is not a common incident, but it can happen. In this case the opposite side was not affected so it will be an easy repair using filler. Alternatively, the manufacturer may replace the part on request.

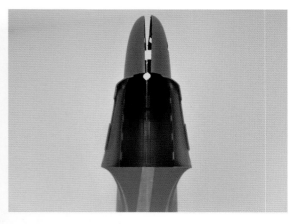

This picture shows that the port side of the fuselage has a warp in the plastic around the nose area. This may cause a problem with fitting the wing if the warp has gone back to the wing root. To get round this problem, fit all the interior bulkheads to the starboard side of the fuselage, then attach the warped port side to the straight side. This will hopefully eliminate the warp.

Building models can be a messy task, especially if you are sanding resin or painting using an airbrush. Spaces used for model making range from a square of the kitchen table, under the stairs, a spare room, roof space, a converted or purpose-built shed, a garage, or a combination of these. Wherever you choose to model, please be aware that some products, as mentioned in Chapter 2 – particularly polyurethane resin dust, or polyester car-body filler – can be carcinogenic, so make sure you have adequate ventilation, use a face mask, and keep your work area tidy. Have consideration for other members of the household who may need to use the space, or who may pick up objects from your bench.

This is what a clean workspace should look like.

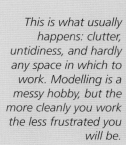

This is what usually happens: clutter, untidiness, and hardly any space in which to work. Modelling is a messy hobby, but the more cleanly you work the less frustrated you will be.

- Selection of sanding sticks, particularly 120 grit to 1200 grit
- Round and square needle files
- Pin vice with a selection of drills
- Scissors
- Methods of clamping parts together, for example pegs, masking tape, rubber bands or clamps
- Cutting mat
- Plastic glue and ultra-thin cement
- Cocktail sticks
- Cotton buds
- Decal setting solutions
- Plastic putty/filler
- Disposable masks

For building more advanced kits or multimedia kits, further tools may be required:

- Clamping tweezers
- Small box-nose pliers with smooth faces
- Etched brass folding tool
- Photo etch scissors
- Various riffler files
- Powered mini drill with speed control with various attachments
- Mini vice
- 6in engineer's ruler
- Dust mask
- Safety glasses
- Superglues, medium and thin
- Five-minute epoxy glue
- PVA glue
- Electronic measuring callipers
- Magnifiers
- Daylight lamp
- Panel scribers
- Riveting tools
- Scribing templates

Not all the items mentioned are absolute must-haves, but some items – such as tweezers for handling etched brass – need to be of high quality, or you will become frustrated when you lose parts because the grip is poor due to cheap manufacture. Side cutters, otherwise known as sprue cutters, also require careful purchase. Xuron do an excellent range of sprue cutters and etch scissors with an accurate clip, while some of the cheaper sprue cutters will tear the plastic instead of cutting through it cleanly.

Eyesight is also worth a mention. Frequently eyesight can change with age, and working with fine etched brass requires good vision and patience. As well as ensuring that you visit the opticians as recommended, your vision can be helped with good lighting and magnifiers. It is surprising how much neater your build can be when you use magnification. This is also true of painting small details.

PAINT BRUSHES

Paint brushes are an important part of your tool kit. For painting small details, such as cockpit instrument panels, fine-point brushes are a must. There are several manufacturers who produce good brushes, including Modelkasten and Army Painter. For covering large areas I would recommend using sign-writers' one-stroke brushes. These are broad, chisel-edged brushes with long hairs, designed to cover in one stroke. Premier Brush Company is a good supplier of this type of brush, and their range includes other brush types that might be useful.

To look after your brushes, keep them clean. If you will not be using them for a while, coat them with linseed oil or a smear of Vaseline, and lie them flat. This will keep the hairs supple and in good condition. Never leave a brush standing on its hairs in thinners or water: doing this can permanently damage the hairs within a short time. With good-quality brushes painting becomes a pleasure.

Even when using a brush, most paints still require a certain amount of thinner to be added. How much will depend upon the viscosity of the chosen paint. Some paints, especially acrylics, work better with a few drops of retarder or flow enhancer in them. When brush painting,

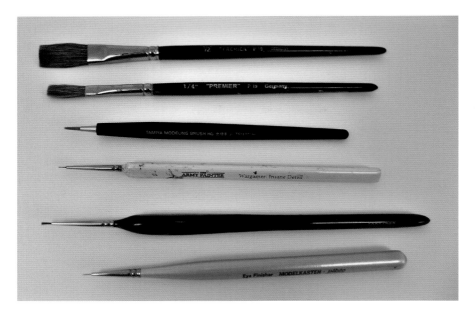

A variety of brushes, from large flats for covering areas, to fine points for fine details. Quality brushes make painting much easier. Note that some brush manufacturers will still use imperial sizes on larger brushes.

as with airbrushing, do not try to cover in one coat. Depending on the colour and how much the paint is thinned, three coats would normally be needed for coverage. When applying the paint, use a brush that fits the scale. Some traditional brush companies still use imperial sizes, whereas other companies use 'triple zero' to denote the finest size, to zero for fine, and then in increasing numerals as the brushes get larger.

AIRBRUSHING

The author's previous book, *Airbrushing Scale Model Aircraft* (The Crowood Press Ltd, 2018), describes in detail the use of airbrush equipment, from purchase and setting up, through training exercises to full paint schemes. In brief, the advice included on airbrushing equipment states that buying a compressor and airbrush package is an investment, and that it is always worth paying for good-quality equipment. Beginners should go to an established or recommended airbrush supplier, who will be able to offer advice, and who will give different options according to what the equipment will be used for. Model shows often have specialist retailers offering compressors and airbrushes, and

they can give advice as to what may be needed. Established modellers who display their work at shows are usually more than happy to offer guidance and share their experience.

In order to operate any airbrush successfully, it is essential to have a constant air supply. It is possible to use compressed air from a car tyre and adapter, or from divers' air tanks, but these will only give a limited supply of constant air before the pressure starts to drop. Some manufacturers supply an airbrush starter set with a can of compressed air, but again, the air pressure will soon start to drop, and you may run out of air just as you come to a critical part of painting, or when you are trying to clean the airbrush. For no more than the cost of half a dozen cans of air you could buy a compressor that is designed specifically for airbrushing.

Bear in mind that compressors that are sold at garages or camping outlets are only designed to inflate air beds or beach toys, and will not run an airbrush.

If possible, try to keep your compressor away from the immediate spraying area, as it takes the air from its surroundings. Airlines are available in plastic or braided material up to ten feet long, which is quite long enough for the compressor to be kept under the workbench.

Not everyone can have a separate location for airbrushing, so having a portable set-up is ideal. The compressor is under the workbench, and the moisture trap and regulator are clamped to the worktop. The airbrush holder is also a micro switch, so when the airbrush is taken off, the compressor will automatically start up.

BONDING PLASTIC

In the early days of plastic model building, the only glue choice would have been a tube of polystyrene cement. Currently the market is filled by many manufacturers producing all kinds of polystyrene glue, fast-setting liquid cement such as Tamiya extra thin or 'Plastic Magic' from Deluxe Materials. A new glue from Revell called Fix-Kit has recently come on to the market, which consists

There is a plethora of glues available. Pictured here is a selection of typical glues required for building multimedia kits.

of an ultraviolet marker and lamp and UV 'Super Kleber', which when used together use ultraviolet light to form the bond.

When applying glues, you will need to use either the supplied applicator or a cheap paint brush. Glues often contain acetone, and give off strong vapours that are irritating and highly flammable, so make sure you use them in a ventilated area. Superglues can be used, but these bond almost instantly, which means you have little time to manoeuvre the parts if this is required; nevertheless they are very useful when bonding different substrates.

Where superglues come into their own is when the modeller is cementing small, delicate items such as pitot heads or external flying surface balance weights, or is reinforcing a joint from the inside.

CLAMPING

Most modern kits are 3D computer-aided designs (CAD). The CAD process makes the kit much easier to build, as the fit of parts is much better than kits from previous decades. If you are working with older kits or those not designed with computers you may find that when, for example, you put wing halves together and then look along the trailing or leading edge, there is a curve to the wing. This can be straightened by gluing the wing together and clamping the wing to a flat surface.

There are numerous different types of model makers' clamp available – for example, from Expo Tools. Remember not to over-tighten clamps, nor to use ones that need excessive strength to operate them, as they can distort the parts you are gluing, leaving a step. Other methods for clamping can be used, such as rubber bands, washing-line pegs or masking tape.

FILLING

The finished surface of your model will reflect what is underneath. Any imperfections, deep scratches, gaps, lumps and bumps will show through painted surfaces, and trying to bury them with paint will not work. Thorough preparation is essential.

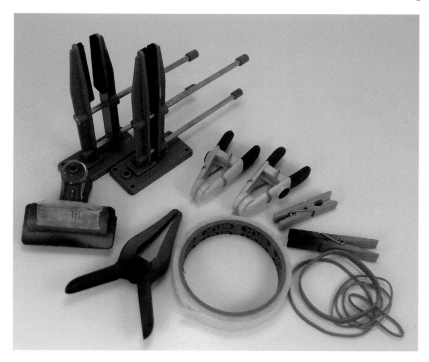

Some form of clamping is essential when building models. All these items are inexpensive and readily available from hobby or hardware stores.

Inspect all surfaces for gaps and imperfections, and lightly mark them with a pencil so you will find them again when filling. You will need to fill gaps on poorly fitting parts as well as sink marks on the visible surface. Sand the surface around any defects before applying the filler, to help blend in the edges of the filled portion.

There are many different types of filler available to modellers – the key thing is to find the right one for the job. Using single-pack putty for a large gap will only work if you apply it in several layered applications, as this type of filler shrinks back and if applied in deep layers will stay soft underneath for a long period. It is better to use a model putty such as Milliput, a two-part epoxy that is kneaded together prior to application. Any excess can be worked away with water.

Some modellers use car-body filler, and for smaller areas it is possible to use baking powder or micro balloons with superglue. It is important to note that some two-pack fillers are carcinogenic, so make sure you wear a mask when rubbing them down. The smaller the scale, the finer the rubbing down should be. Use a file or sanding stick to rub down seams, joints or excess glue marks. Firm favourites amongst modellers are the sponge sanding sticks used by manicure technicians. There are various grades, from 100 grit up to 1,200 grit for general sanding, and 3,000 grit to 12,000 grit for polishing and buffing. The softer sponge sanders will allow you to ride over small raised details such as rivets or small vents without damaging them.

Please be aware that some metal finishes are so fine they will show up scratches from rubbing down if you have used too coarse a sanding stick or finishing pad. For small amounts of filler start with 180 grit and finish off with 240 grit or finer if doing metal finishes. Once the primer is on, you will have another chance to correct any flaws before putting on the finish coats.

Small gaps can be filled using a high-build primer. This product usually has micro fillers included, which help to bridge the gap. Apply with a brush, wait approximately fifteen minutes, and then, using a cotton bud soaked in rubbing alcohol, remove the excess, leaving the gap filled with primer. This method is preferable where the gap is close to raised detail that you don't want to damage when rubbing down. White correction ink can also be used in this way.

SCRIBING/RE-SCRIBING

Having assembled your aircraft model, and filled and sanded the inevitable gaps, seams and

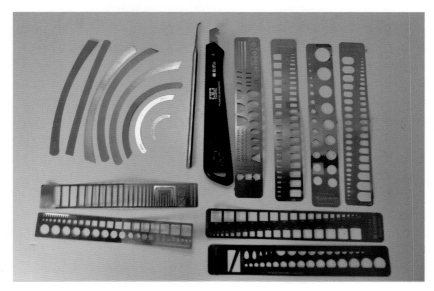

Scribers and scribing templates come in many shapes and sizes. Some of the shapes can also be used as a mask when airbrushing.

imperfections, you may have lost some recessed or raised seams on the fuselage or wings. There may also be missing panel markings that you want to display. These faults can all be revived or corrected by using a scriber and scribing templates. It shouldn't be too difficult to source scribers as there are many companies, including model kit manufacturers, producing them. As with any tool, if used correctly they will produce good results, but they do require patience and a steady hand.

If you are using a scriber for the first time, spend a little time practising on a piece of plastic card or an old kit. Start by using light pressure: the idea is to cut a 'V' into the plastic at a 90-degree angle to the surface. If you apply too much pressure you may force the scriber into the plastic too far, causing a raised edge on each side of the seam. It helps if you understand the type of plastic the kit manufacturer has used, as there are different plastics used for models, some soft and some hard. Each type will react differently to scribing.

You can also use a scriber to help remove moulded-on flying controls, such as flaps, which are to be replaced with etched brass ones, or elevators moulded in a neutral position where a change of angle is desired. The Tamiya heavy-duty

scriber is good for these tasks. Adding or repairing access panels can be done using scribing templates which can be purchased from hobby stores or from online suppliers. For curved seams on a tapering fuselage, a straight edge will be of no use, but Hasegawa produce a set of curves of different radii. One of these should match up to the seam you require.

RAISED AND RECESSED RIVETING

Historically, kit manufacturers frequently moulded raised riveting and panel lines on to model aircraft, though it was often overscale and inaccurate. This trend disappeared in favour of recessed riveting and engraved panel lines. This can look convincing if they are in scale, but of course the rivets are not raised, where in some cases they should be. Currently manufacturers are using both raised and recessed rivets, combined with moulding an 'oil-canning' effect. This effect can be seen on many World War II aircraft, where the skins look as if they are ballooned out, and the rivet runs are slightly recessed.

Replacing raised rivets can be done in two ways. The easier is to use transfer rivets. At least

A mix of raised riveting, flush or recessed riveting, and the 'oil canning' effect of the skins lower down on the fuselage.

two companies make these, the foremost being HGW from the Czech Republic, and Archer Fine Transfers from the USA. The process is similar to the application of decal markings, but instead of using inks they use resin, giving a raised rivet in single or multiple lines. There are different-shaped access panels and hinge lines available, and HGW also do complete kits for certain aircraft in 1/72, 1/48 and 1/32 scale.

The second way is to use fine brass rivets available from modelmotorcars.com in the USA, or resin cast rivets from CMK in the Czech Republic. These are not very practical to complete a model aircraft as you would need thousands of them, but

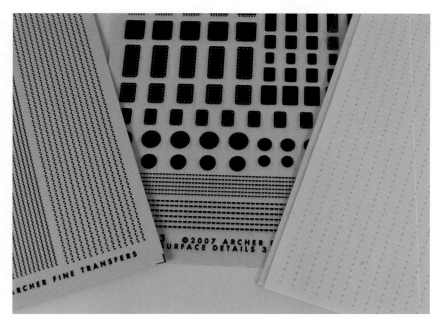

Transfer rivets: they come in most common scales, and applied in this form it is possible to cover areas rapidly. They are very effective once painted.

Pounce wheels can be used on plastic. Plastic kit manufacturers will use different plastics, some hard and some soft. Make a test first to get the feel of how much pressure needs to be applied for the required effect. Indentations can be used to repair areas or to create new rivet runs.

A beading tool, which can be used to simulate countersunk riveting. Patience is required, and it is recommended to work on one small section at a time.

they can be useful in isolated areas of larger scale models, such as engines or undercarriage bays.

Some kits will have engraved panel lines and no riveting at all. It could be that you have lost some rivet detail while sanding. If you want to show riveting details when this applies there are tools to help. Pounce wheels, which are traditional sign-writers' or artists' tools, are wheels held in a fork and handle, with evenly spaced teeth. These follow a design drawn on paper, piercing through the paper and allowing chalk powder to be rubbed through the holes, thus transferring the design on to the underlying surface. Pounce wheels can be applied directly to plastic using a stainless-steel template as a guide. The points on the wheel pierce the plastic leaving an indentation. Pounce wheels come in different sizes and are gauged by teeth per inch. The gauge can be matched up to rivet lines in different scales.

Another handy tool for countersunk riveting is a beading tool. It comes complete with handle and twelve different sizes of countersunk tips. Once the correct rivet size is selected, insert the appropriate tip in the handle and test on a piece of plastic from the kit. The inside surface of the wing or fuselage is ideal. Doing a test on the kit plastic will give you a good indication of how much pressure to use when completing your rivet runs.

Chapter Two

What Is Multimedia?

'Multimedia' is the term used for accessories produced to improve model kits, or to enhance a complete kit made up from various materials. This chapter provides an explanation of the differences between these media, how they are produced, the best ways to work them, and what glues are useable.

ETCHED BRASS: WHERE THE PROCESS STARTS

Etched brass and nickel silver are widely used in model kits now. Both allow very detailed small parts to be produced. For example, model throttle levers would look overscale if manufactured in plastic. Use of brass and nickel-silver detailing is not restricted to small parts, however, as large assemblies can also be produced, such as landing flaps.

To demonstrate the process, this chapter follows a CorelDRAW computer file produced by Scalewarship Ltd, from drawing through to production. The etched brass fret is later used on a model, as described in Chapter 7.

Before the advent of computer technology, the required design was produced by hand as a technical drawing. Today the process is usually done on computer in a program such as AutoCAD or CorelDRAW. The computer drawing is usually done in three layers using different colours: red, half etch from the front; blue, half etch from the back; and black, for a complete cut right through the material. The drawn blue and red 'instructions' are useful to provide raised or engraved detail, a process often referred to as 'relief etch'.

Once all the parts are drawn up, they are arranged into a fret. This is done to maximize the number of parts obtained from one area of the finished material. When the efficient fret design is complete, the parts are 'tabbed up' to the frame. Tabbing holds everything together while it is put through the etching process. Once complete, the fret design computer file is sent to the etchers to have the photo tooling made.

A simple photo tool is like an old-fashioned photograph negative, except there are two films, a 'back' and a 'front' film. Both films have the full etched and full thickness detail, the 'front' has the half-etch front detail (red) and the 'back' has the half-etch back detail (blue). These are perfectly lined up with each other either manually

Etched brass is very useful when illustrating small details, such as these throttle box and levers from the Mosquito in Chapter 6.

Landing flaps are commonly made in etched brass set for aircraft kits. Some can be quite complex, like these flaps from a 1/32-scale Focke-Wulf 190. Small folds, curves and embossing are needed to complete these flaps. These can be seen completed in Chapter 8.

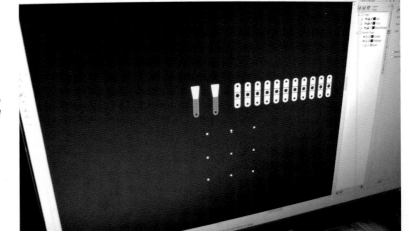

Using a CorelDRAW program, the parts required are drawn up and assembled in groups.

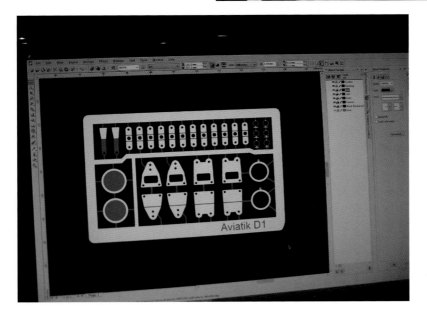

The final drawing. All the parts are drawn up and grouped. They are then put together on a fret and tabbed up. This is to stop all the parts falling off when going through the etching process. The drawing is then sent to the etchers as a CDR file for processing.

and by eye, or by using registration marks. The metal is then selected and cut to size. It is then carefully cleaned with alcohol wipes before being put through a machine which 'micro-etches' the surface and gives an automatic rinse.

Once the sheet is dry it is then coated with photoresist (a photosensitive substance which when exposed to UV light, loses its resistance to acid) on both sides. Once the metal is coated with resist it is placed between the two photo films and exposed to UV light. Where the light passes through the clear areas on the film the resist will harden, and where there are black areas on the film the light is shielded, and the resist will stay soft.

The metal is then put through a developer where the soft resist is dissolved, and the hardened resist remains. The metal is then sprayed on both sides with etchant (traditionally a strong acid or mordant), and where the developer has washed away the resist, the exposed metal is dissolved away leaving the actual part but still covered with resist. This must be removed using resist stripper before exposing the finished product. Some of the larger manufacturers will have fully auto-mated machines for this process, and have the capability of producing pre-coloured photo etch such as seat belts and instrument panels, which removes the need to hand paint fine details on these items.

The photo tool is made using this machine. The dark room is on the other side of the door. The file is processed through this and comes out in this room as a negative, front and back.

This is what a photo tool looks like. Detail from the front is on the left, and detail from the rear is on the right.

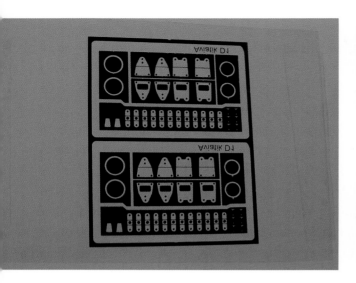 

ABOVE LEFT: *The two films are now on top of each other, perfectly lined up and taped on two sides to stop the films moving out of line.*

ABOVE RIGHT: *Once the brass has been selected the sheet is cleaned with alcohol and put through a micro-etch machine. This machine micro-etches the surface and then washes it as it comes out. It is then dried in an oven before going on to have the photo resist applied.*

ABOVE LEFT: *The photo resist is sensitive to UV light, so the process is done under a yellow light. The sheet is fed into the machine and the resist is applied on both top and bottom surfaces at the same time by the rollers. This picture has been filtered for better viewing.*

ABOVE RIGHT: *The sheet is cut down to size and placed between the two photo-tool films. This is then exposed to ultra-violet light for five seconds. Please note this picture has been taken under yellow lighting so has been filtered for clarity.*

The photo resist now shows up as blue on the brass sheet. This is then put through a developer, which exposes the image on to both sides of the brass. This is then dried and inspected for any defects.

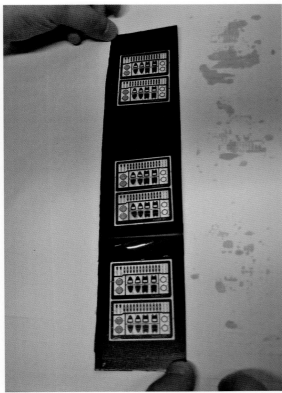

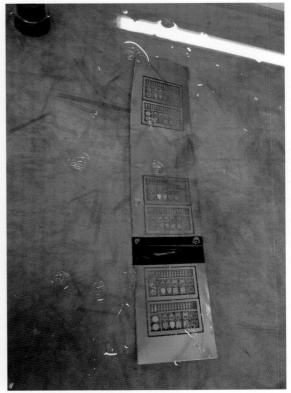

The sheet is now put through the etching process where the developer has washed away the soft resist: the exposed metal is dissolved away leaving the actual part but still covered with resist.

Finally the sheet is placed into a bath of resist stripper, rinsed and dried. A final inspection is done before it is wrapped up and sent out to the customer.

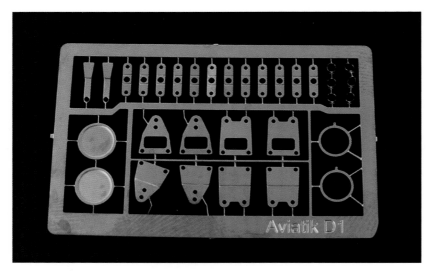

The final product is ready to go. Note that in this state it is easy to damage very fragile parts, as shown in the top right of this image. Parts like this are worth over-producing, in this case doubling the quantity as only three were required. Unwanted items can then act as spares.

Tools

The most commonly used tools when using etched brass are the following:

- Sharp knife
- 'Hold and fold' type tool
- Box-nosed pliers with smooth faces
- Flat-nosed tweezers
- Fine-pointed tweezers
- Single-edge razor blade or Stanley blade
- Paper embossing tools

Cutting etched parts from the fret needs to be done on a hard surface with a sharp knife. For very small pieces it is best to place a piece of masking tape, sticky side up, under the fret. This will stop the part bouncing away and being lost when it is cut through. If etched parts are dropped on to

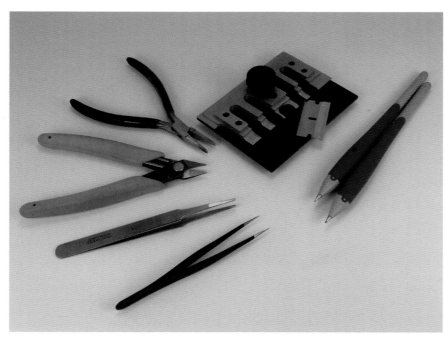

A typical range of useful tools for working with etched brass.

carpet and land on their edge, they are very difficult to find. Most tabs on an etch fret will be half etched, so that if you place the knife blade as close as possible to the part you are removing and at an angle, you will cut through more accurately, leaving very little stub to clean up.

Once the part has been separated from the fret there will usually be a small stub that will need filing down. Larger stubs can be trimmed off using photo-etch scissors. Hold the part in smooth box-nosed pliers or flat-nosed tweezers when filing, and use gentle filing strokes.

Folding Brass

If you intend using a lot of etched brass fittings, then it's worth the investment of buying a purposely designed tool. Such tools are made in sizes starting at approximately 2sq in, going through various dimensions up to 14in long (designed for the model railway market). A 4in folding tool is adequate for most model aircraft etched brass, but if you intend to use 1/32-scale Lancaster or Flying Fortress flaps then a larger tool may be necessary.

Folding etched brass requires careful thought and needs to be worked in the correct sequence, especially when there are multiple folds to be made. Where parts have fold lines etched on the surface, folds are generally folded towards them. This is not universally true, as mistakes can be made by designers, or the designs are deliberately prepared that way. The etched brass instructions will include a computer drawing, usually with symbols identifying what is to be done with the part – for example, a curved arrow indicates a fold. It is worth spending some time thinking through the process before committing because instruction drawings can be confusing.

Studying the part and any adjoining parts should determine which way it is intended the folds should be made. For example, folding a narrow 3mm-wide strip with a fold line down the length really needs to be done using an etch folding tool or clamp, or there is a possibility it will end up as a wrinkled strip. Where there may

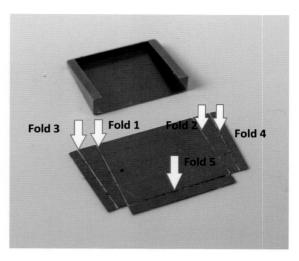

Where multiple folds are needed, always start with the inner folds first. If you start on the outside you will find it difficult to fold the inner ones last, and may damage those already made.

be five or more folds on one piece, study the part and imagine how you would fold it, before you start to fold. Start on the innermost folds first, then work outwards. Many of the small cockpit components can be folded using small, smooth-faced box pliers or smooth-faced flat tweezers. Some folds can be done using a metal ruler as a clamp and a single-edged blade to make the fold.

Embossing Brass

Some photo-etch producers have introduced embossing into their instructions to produce a 3D effect. The usual indicator for use of this technique is half etch on the inside face of what is to be embossed – for example, a long strip or a dome in a door pane. The symbol used in the instructions for embossing can be a ballpoint pen nib or a steel ball. Embossing pens are readily available in the arts and craft market, initially designed for paper, but ideal for etched brass.

Whatever is to be embossed, try to use a tool suitable for the size of the completed mark – for example, a ballpoint pen for a small strip, or a ball bearing for a large dome. Place the part on to a piece of rubber, making sure the rubber has some 'give' in it, or on to a cutting mat with the

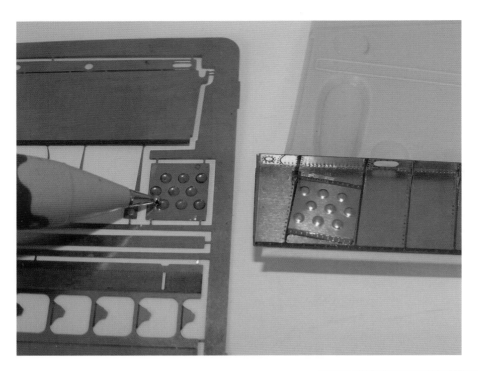

Embossing brass can be achieved by using paper embossing tools (like the one shown). For very small, narrow channels a ballpoint pen can be used.

half-etched part facing up. Then, using the appropriate tool, apply pressure to the half-etched area in regular movements. Stop now and then to check the front face for the desired effect. There is no need to anneal the brass, as the half-etched area will be thin enough to emboss without softening the brass.

Rolling Brass and Annealing

To put a curve in a piece of brass there are specialist tools available from numerous model tool suppliers. They consist of wood or metal rollers and a base, with corresponding channels into which to form the brass. Sometimes it will be necessary to anneal the brass first. To anneal brass, heat the brass up until it glows red, then let it cool down, or quench it in water. Both methods work well.

Once this has been done the brass is very pliable and will easily conform to a round surface. Without annealing you can manually curve a piece of brass by placing it on to a cutting mat, selecting a round metal or wooden rod, and placing it on to the brass. Then roll the rod backwards and

This tool is called the Brass-Assist, and is used for forming curves in brass. The curves are made by using the formed channels and steel rods. On the reverse of the tool there is a rubber pad which is useful for embossing or forming curves by rolling brass between the rubber and the supplied rods. Other suitable tools can be used as rods, such as wood dowels or drill bits.

SUPERGLUE SAFETY

Cyanoacrylate, otherwise known as 'superglue', is a strong glue used in many applications, including medical. This type of glue, if used correctly, will give excellent bonding. It has rapid, medium and slow drying capabilities. It can be activated instantly with the use of an accelerator. Many superglues give off vapours that are irritants, but a vapourless superglue is available.

The main issue to be aware of is that superglue will bond your fingers together instantly: if this happens there are superglue removers available from superglue manufacturers. Always keep a bottle to hand, but should you find yourself without any, an alternative method of removing the glue is to immerse your fingers in warm, soapy water, gently prising them apart.

Be aware that thin superglue, if spilt in quantity on to a carpet or clothing, will form an instant lump and get hot as it sets. If you mop up spilt superglue with kitchen towel, the towel can get hot and give off irritating vapours.

forwards, applying light pressure. This will compress the upper surface and stretch the undersurface, forming a curve. Thin brass will curve quickly, thicker brass will take a little longer.

Bonding
Bonding etched brass can be achieved using the following:

Superglue
Epoxy glue
Solder
Clear coats
PVA

It is unlikely that you will need to use solder when putting scale model aircraft together, but it would provide structural strength. With the very fine details in model aircraft etch sets, soldering skill will need to be at an appropriate level. Most of the etched brass components will be small and can be glued in place with superglue. Larger components, such as bulkheads, bonded on to plastic may need a slow-drying superglue or a five-minute epoxy glue. The slower drying time will enable you to manoeuvre the part into the correct place. If used correctly, superglue will give a solid bond. The smaller components are best held in place with tweezers. Then, using a piece of fine wire, pick up a little thin superglue and touch the base of the part being glued. Capillary action will leach around the part, bonding it securely.

If superglue accidently gets splashed on to etched brass, it can be removed by holding the part with tweezers into the flame of a candle. The flame will burn off all the glue, but the part will have soot deposits left on it, so will then need to be cleaned up before reapplying. There are also small bottles of superglue remover available from superglue manufacturers. Apply with an old brush, and wait for the superglue to go soft, then clean up with soapy water. Superglue can also be used as a filler in conjunction with baking powder or a specifically designed powder.

If you are using pre-coloured photo etch, such as that used to denote an instrument panel, instrument bezels may need to be glued on. The safest way to do this is to use a clear coat or PVA. Lay the panel on a flat surface, carefully locate the bezel, and hold it in place with a pair of tweezers; then with a small amount of clear coat on a fine brush, touch the edge of the bezel and let capillary action leach the clear coat around the bezel. If it is an instrument face within the bezel, then a

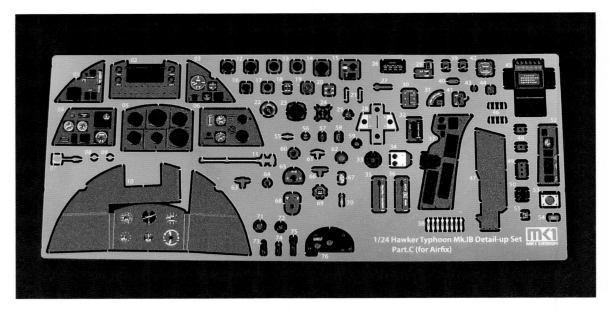

A pre-coloured, photo-etched instrument panel. Notice that many of the parts will need to be laminated. Careful work with superglue or the use of a clear coat will be needed to bond these together. The disadvantages to this type of instrument panel are that the printed colour can easily be chipped off, or the colours may not be quite right. The photographic process has made the front faces lighter, but even accounting for this, they appear much too grey instead of the black they should be.

clear coat can be applied to the face: this will give the glass effect and bond the bezel in place. Some pre-coloured photo etch comes with an adhesive backing that doesn't require any gluing.

CASTING, SILICON AND POLYURETHANE RESIN

Polyurethane resin is very popular with aftermarket manufacturers for producing a three-dimensional part which cannot be reproduced in photo etch, such as a wheel. Virtually anything can be cast, from a small component to a full kit. The process starts with a 'master'. This can be made by hand, or designed in a CAD program on computer, then printed in three dimensions (3D). Depending on the type of material and printing machine, 3D printing can leave steps or marks in the printed article as it builds it up in layers. If such faults are visible on the printed component to be used as a master, these will need to be corrected before

The six cylinders supplied in the HpH kit had poorly formed seams on both sides of the cylinders. It would have been possible to clean them all up carefully, but some were in a worse state than others. So for the purpose of illustration, it was decided to make one good one, then make a mould and cast six more.

the part is sent for casting, otherwise the same steps or marks will be reproduced in all the castings. These marks can be eradicated using filler primer or a dedicated material such as XTC-3D by Smooth-On. This is a self-levelling coating that will not leave any brush marks.

To demonstrate the casting process, two simple moulds were made: an engine cylinder from a 1/18-scale engine, and some access panels on a F4U-1D Corsair. Mould making for casting purposes can be complex, especially with multi-part moulds. Only the basic mould types will be dealt with here, which most competent modellers can easily achieve with a little guidance. The simplest way to make a mould is to make a 'dam' into which you pour some silicone rubber. Children's building blocks can be used for the purpose, or some very basic shapes can be pressed into a putty.

Be aware that if you copy kit parts and try to sell what you have produced you may be in breach of copyrights, so the techniques described here are intended for the modeller's own use only.

The interior of the rear fuselage was accurately moulded, including the pressed access panels. This is a good opportunity for a basic mould demonstration, and these panels will be used on a future project.

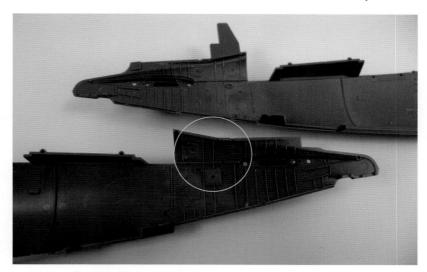

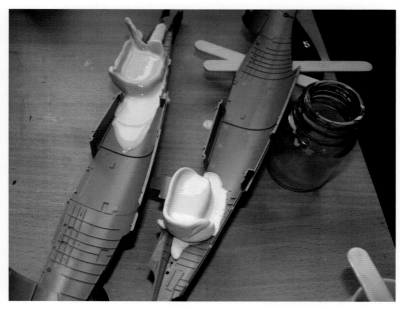

White Tak was used to form a dam around the areas required. This was then filled with a mix of silicone rubber and left to cure. Any spillages or overflow will cure in the same way as the required mould and can be peeled away when cured. After removing the mould and excess silicon, the model parts were washed with warm soapy water to remove any traces of silicon.

The result, shown here, is the basic mould and the resin panels. The panels have been primed to highlight the detail.

The engine cylinder master was taken from the multi-media Aviatik Berg D.1 kit (the full build is described in Chapter 7). The supplied cylinders had some awkward seams as a likely result of a worn original mould. One cylinder was in better condition than the rest, so this one was cleaned up and used as a master. The Corsair access panels were accurately moulded on the inside surface of the kit's fuselage. By making a mould of this area the modeller can cut out the plastic panels and replace them with the moulded resin ones in the open position. This means making a dam around some awkward curves and protrusions. White Tak is a useful material for this purpose, as it can be easily moulded around the required areas, and then filled with a mix of silicon rubber. This type of open mould is suitable for one-off castings, where a mix of resin is just smeared into the mould with a mixing stick.

HEALTH AND SAFETY

Silicon rubber and polyurethane resins are chemicals that need appropriate health and safety precautions. The moulding process can be very messy, so only attempt to make moulds using these if you are confident in using and understanding what the issues are. Be sure to read the manufacturer's safety data sheets carefully, and use appropriate personal protection equipment, as indicated in those instructions.

Casting Using a Vacuum Chamber

If you are considering casting some of your own masters that have undercuts or complex detail, you will need to use a vacuum chamber. A complete vacuum kit can be purchased from around £120.

The silicon rubber used to make the mould will need to be de-gassed, as will the polyurethane resin. Air bubbles will otherwise be visible in the moulded piece and will spoil the areas where it is intended the undercuts or fine details are to be shown. If the master is hollow, then this will need to be filled before placing it into a vacuum chamber, otherwise once the hollow master is placed into a vacuum chamber, when de-gassed it will implode or distort.

Once the engine cylinder for the 1/18-scale Aviatik Berg was prepared and primed, it was bonded on to a 2in plastic card base with a small spot of superglue. A hot glue gun would have worked equally well. The article to be moulded

must be bonded down for two reasons: the bond area forms the entrance hole to the finished mould, and the item would otherwise float in the liquid silicon. Next, four walls of plastic card were built up around the cylinder, using superglue (or a hot glue gun), allowing at least a 5mm distance around the cylinder, and twice the height of the cylinder. The two times height measure is required as the silicon will rise when being de-gassed. All the joints were carefully sealed to ensure no silicon could escape.

If you wish to do a lot of casting, you will need a casting set-up which typically consists of vacuum pump, de-gassing chamber and electronic scales for measuring small quantities of liquids. In addition to this you will need mixing cups, mixing 'lollypop' sticks and gloves.

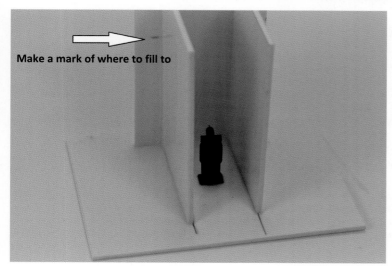

Make a mark of where to fill to

When making a box around the item that is to be cast (the master), it is advisable to leave a minimum of 5 to 10mm around the object, otherwise the walls of the mould may distort when filled with resin. Notice the mark that indicates the level to which to fill. This ensures you cover the object with enough silicon, which as with the side walls, should be between 5 to 10mm.

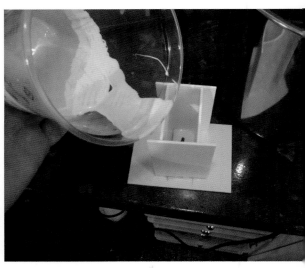

ABOVE LEFT: *After mixing the silicon, de-gas in the chamber. Keep an eye on the liquid as it will boil up and may overflow. If it gets close to the top, let in some air, which will settle it down again, then continue de-gassing.*

ABOVE RIGHT: *Pour the de-gassed silicon slowly over the object until you reach the fill mark.*

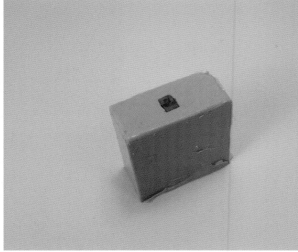

ABOVE LEFT: *Place the filled mould in the de-gassing chamber and de-gas, keeping an eye on the liquid as it can still boil up and overflow. If you have undercuts and hollows you may need to add a little more silicon and de-gas again.*

ABOVE RIGHT: *After approximately twenty-four hours the silicon should be cured, and you can remove the plastic walls and base. The master should be exposed, and by gently squeezing and pushing, it should come out. If the master is stubborn, and at the first pull it usually is, then you may need to put a cut in the mould to help it out.*

The newly cast cylinders at the front have been primed for clarity, and the originals at the rear for comparison.

Mixing Silicon Rubber

Silicon rubber comes in many different hardness levels or durometer (resistance to indentation), which can be expressed in a scale known as 'Shore'. The scale measures a range from 0 (extra soft) to 100 (extra hard). Small, fragile parts are better suited to a softer Shore; the moulds made in this chapter are at Shore 22.

Once the master is prepared and mounted in its mould box, the silicon should be mixed. Mixing silicon requires scales to ensure accurate ingredient measures, but the ratios of each ingredient will vary according to which manufacturer has produced them, as does the curing and working time. Once mixed and before putting it into the mould box, the silicon will need to be de-gassed. Because the silicon mix will 'boil up' during de-gassing it is best to mix in a pot bigger than the quantity of the ingredients to prevent any overflow going into the chamber. During de-gassing keep an eye on the silicon, and let some air out of the chamber as it boils up to stop it flowing over the edge of the pot. Continue de-gassing until the silicon stops bubbling.

Once the silicon is fully de-gassed, pour it slowly into the mould until the master is covered by at least 5mm, then place the mould back into the vacuum chamber and de-gas again. After de-gassing, leave the mould to cure for twenty-four hours before removing the walls and master. Simple masters will come out of the mould easily, but masters with undercuts may be more stubborn and may need to be cut from the new silicon mould.

Mixing Resin

Before mixing the resin, prepare the mould by putting a 1in-wide piece of clear sticky tape half attached and half loose around the top of the mould. This is to act as a dam when pouring in the resin. Remember to seal any cuts you have made to the mould with a piece of tape.

A polyurethane resin mix is usually fifty parts resin to fifty parts activator. Casting resin can have a mix working time of two to seven minutes before it starts to cure. Make sure to shake the resin well and let it settle before pouring, then, as with silicon, pour slowly and tap the mould to coax out any air.

Swiftly place the mould into the vacuum chamber and de-gas. When using a fast cast resin, you may need to mix the resin, pour into the mould and de-gas in the vacuum chamber in one go. If lots of air is released from the mould, then the dam of resin on the top should flow back into the mould.

Basic Manual Casting

Parts that have a simple shape can be cast manually without the use of a vacuum chamber. The process of making a box to prepare the mould is the same as outlined above. The silicon needs to be mixed slowly to prevent the introduction of air. Also, the mix should be poured slowly into the mould box so that no air is trapped in undercuts or fine detail. Make sure you cover the master by at least 5mm. Once the mould is covered, tap the box a little to coax any air out to the surface.

Leave the mould to cure for twenty-four hours before you remove the plastic walls and the master. As indicated above, you may need to cut the mould if the master is difficult to remove. Prepare the mould by putting a 1in clear sticky

Putting a Sellotape dam around the top allows for air pockets to rise, a process aided by some gentle tapping of the mould. The tape also gives you a purchase when removing the item from the mould.

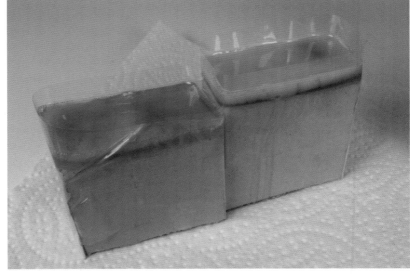

After approximately one and a half minutes the resin will start to change colour and start to cure, getting hot as it does so. After thirty minutes, as long as there is no heat still being produced, the part can be taken out of the mould.

Pulling the casting from the mould. This mould has had a small cut put in the top section to aid the removal of the casting. A mould with undercuts and fine detail will only last for twenty-five to thirty pulls before it starts to break down.

tape 'half and half' around the top of the mould to form the dam needed for pouring in the resin, and cover any cuts made to the mould with a piece of tape. Remember the working and curing times of the mix you are preparing.

Make sure you shake the resin well and let it settle before pouring. Pour slowly, and tap to release any trapped air bubbles.

THREE-DIMENSIONAL PRINTING

Technology is always bringing us something new, and the latest in the field of model making is three-dimensional printing (3Dp). 3Dp is a complex topic and merits its own instruction manuals. Several are already published, including the following: *Make: Getting Started with 3D Printing* by Wallach, Kloski and Kloski; *3D Printing for Dummies (2nd edition)*, Horne and Hauseman; and *The 3D Printing Handbook, Technologies, Design and Applications*, Redwood, Schoffer and Garret. For the purpose of this book we will cover two types of 3Dp machine that can be operated within a small business, from a home workshop or garage.

3Dp has been growing rapidly in recent years. Initially it was used only in large-scale manufacturing, but hobby companies are now using 3Dp as a way of producing masters for plastic kit production, and aftermarket companies use 3Dp masters for additional detail sets. Some companies are building up catalogues of 'off the shelf' items for modellers. Shapeways is one such company providing a 3Dp service.

The process starts with a computer-aided design drawing (CAD). There are many CAD programs to choose from – some examples are *Fusion 360* by Autodesk, *SolidWorks:* Dassault Systemes@, *SketchUp*: @Last Software, and *Rhino*: Robert McNeel & Associates. Most take some time and practice to master.

Shapes are constructed in three dimensions using a wide variety of draughting and sculpting tools. For those who want to know more, there are some basic instructions available on the internet in PDF or tutorial format, or books such as *AutoCAD for Dummies:* Fane, or *The CAD Guidebook*: Schoonmaker.

Once completed, the design can be used for 3Dp, computer numerical control (CNC) laser cutting, or other production methods. There are bureaus or private individuals you can approach to have designs drawn up and printed for you – however, these can be expensive as one-off projects.

For those who can use CAD programs, 3D printers can be purchased at a relatively low cost. FDM (fused deposition modelling) is a technology commonly used in desktop 3D printers, making them clean and simple to use. These machines use thermoplastic polymers in a filament form. The printer follows a pre-determined path, melting the filament as it goes and distributing it to build up the object. The difficulty with this type of printing is that, depending on the settings and shape, when finished, the object produced may have a series of ridges. These can be treated with XTC-3D, a two-pack self-levelling filler that can be sanded and primed, or by using an aerosol filler primer.

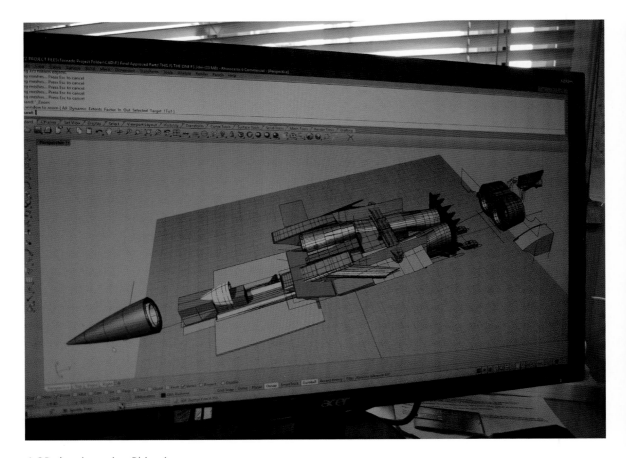

A 3D drawing using Rhino in progress.

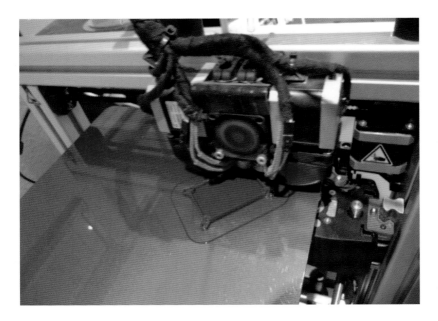

The FDM printer has started the printing process; it will take approximately one hour to complete the print.

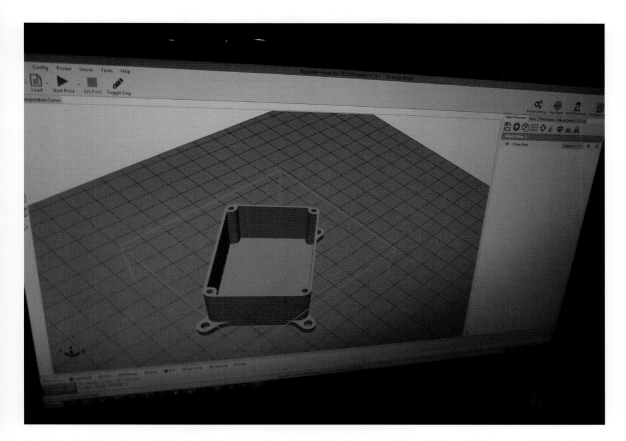

An Alibre design of a small electronic box, now in a Repetier program and ready for printing on an FDM printer.

FDM machines can be purchased from a few hundred pounds, and are an ideal start-up facility for a beginner – but be aware that machines at the lower end of the market are limited in what they can produce. There is a wide range of filament materials available; some examples are polylactic acid (PLA), acrylonitrile butadiene styrene (ABS), and high-impact polystyrene (HIPS), the same plastic as is used in conventional injection-moulded kits.

Formlabs 'Form 2 SLA' machine is more advanced; it uses a process called stereolithography (SLA). SLA printing uses photopolymer resin and a UV laser to progressively build up the object. With Form 2, the build-up is inverted. A moving platform lowers so that it just touches the clear floor of a tank of UV-sensitive resin. It then moves upwards one layer, drawing liquid resin underneath, and after it has moved up, the laser 'writes' the first bottom layer, curing a sliver of resin between the floor of the tank and the platform. The platform then rises, pulling the cured resin off the tank floor, then returns to the next layer position. The next layer bonds to the first.

The process is then repeated until the last layer of the object is deposited and the object built. After the programme is complete, the item is put into isopropyl alcohol to wash off any uncured resin, and further curing with UV light hardens the material.

SLA printing produces a smooth 'ready to go' surface. In the past, SLA printing was very expensive and consequently its use was limited to larger businesses, but as the technology has improved, machinery and resin costs have reduced so a complete Formlabs 'Form 2' set-up can be purchased for £3,500, which is within reach of most small businesses.

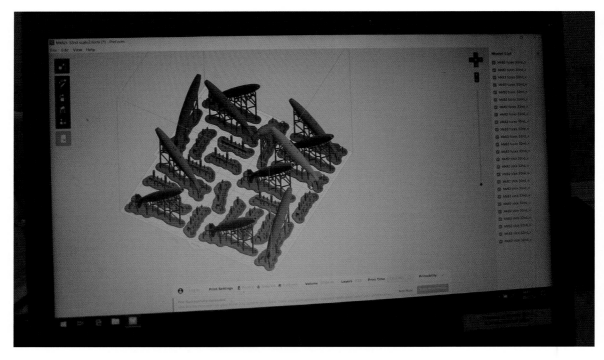

This file is for twelve MK82 bombs and accessories, ready to be loaded up to the printer.

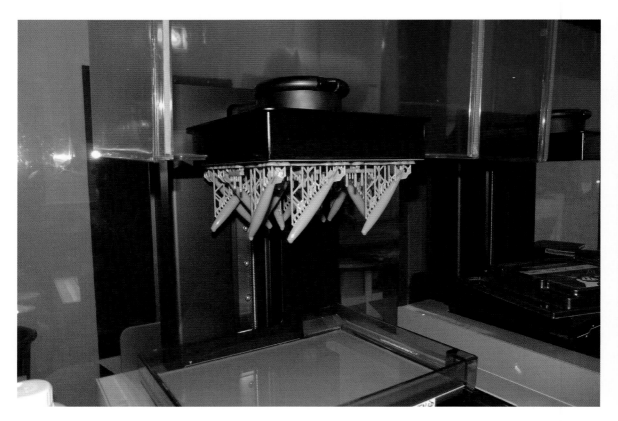

Seven hours later the print is finished. The drips visible on the bombs will disappear when washed with isopropyl alcohol.

The finished item. No further preparation is required, other than removal of the mounts and the application of paint primer.

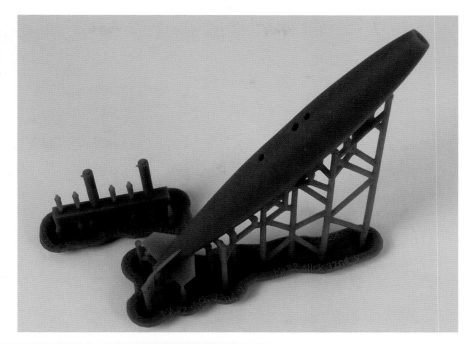

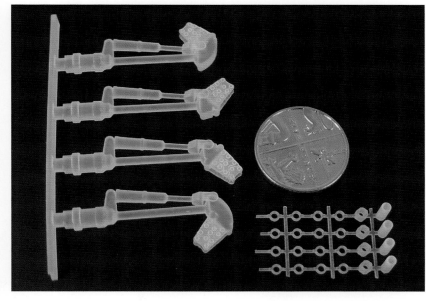

1/32-scale Westland Lynx rotor arms in the folded position, together with some fittings associated with the blade supports. These were printed on a Projet HD 3500 Max at a bureau. This printer is capable of much finer detail, including small tubes and rings, and at far greater accuracy.

Before bonding or painting 3D prints, make sure there is no residue left on them. Such residue may look like a fine sugar or feel like a waxy substance. If any is found, wash the item with warm, soapy water and set it aside to dry. Successful bonding of 3D prints will vary according to the material used in printing. For PLA (polylactic acid) or ABS (acrylonitrile butadiene styrene), acetone or a strong paint thinner will bond with an invisible seam. Superglue will also create a bond, but in some circumstances may be too brittle. The supplier of the prints should be able to give you information as to the best glue to use.

Chapter Three

Hints, Tips and Pitfalls

Before going on to assembling individual aircraft there are four main areas to consider when adding detail to model aircraft:

- Cockpits
- Undercarriage and wheel bays
- Flaps
- Engines

These are the most common components for additional detailing, but there are many more minor parts that can be improved in detail should you wish, such as brass gun barrels and pitot heads, and exhausts. These are generally straightforward replacements of kit parts. Other parts available include replacement flying controls. These are used where the kit manufacturer moulds the rudder, ailerons and elevators on to the wing and tail surfaces in the neutral position. If the modeller wishes to have them in a different position, the moulded-on controls must be removed and replaced with resin aftermarket parts.

Research is an important part of detailing. An example where a common mistake is easily identified by thorough research is the positioning of flaps on a Spitfire model. You will rarely see a Spitfire stationary on the ground with the flaps down, unless they are in that position for maintenance purposes. They are lowered by compressed air, which means that when stationary they are either up or down, never halfway. Flaps on other aircraft are hydraulic, so when the engines are shut down the loss of pressure can result in the flaps creeping down.

There are thousands of books and internet sites where you can research the most common aircraft. Model forums are a good source of information shared by experienced modellers. It's even possible to download maintenance or parts manuals for little or no cost. Parts manuals have excellent diagrams, which may help with knowledge on the model you may be working on.

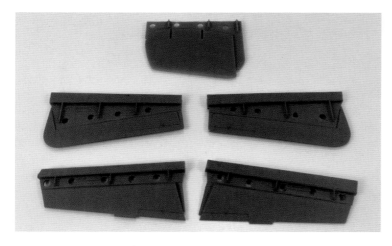

A typical set of separate flying controls. At the top is a rudder for a DC-3 Dakota; the lower ones are ailerons and elevators for the Airfix English Electric Canberra.

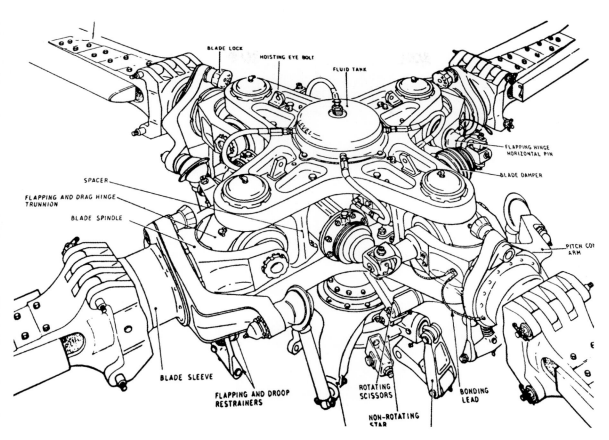

BLADE LOCK

HOISTING EYE BOLT

FLUID TANK

FLAPPING HINGE
HORIZONTAL PIN

BLADE DAMPER

SPACER

FLAPPING AND DRAG HINGE
TRUNNION

BLADE SPINDLE

PITCH CO⌐
ARM

BLADE SLEEVE

FLAPPING AND DROOP
RESTRAINERS

ROTATING
SCISSORS

NON-ROTATING
STAR

BONDING
LEAD

A page from the Westland Wessex Maintenance Manual *showing the component parts of a helicopter rotor head. These are ideal for scratch building or applying extra detail to a basic kit part.*

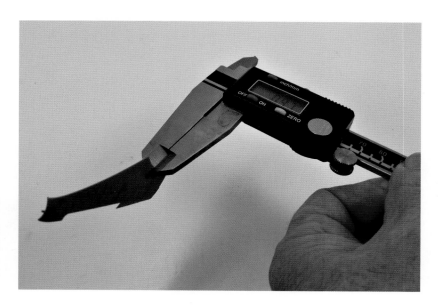

One of the cowlings from the Tamiya 1/32-scale Spitfire, which measures 0.47mm thick. It is easy to see the slight transparency of the material, with the internal framework showing through.

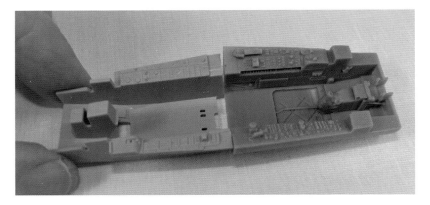

These two cockpits show quite a difference in width. On the left is the plastic one from the kit, and on the right is a resin cockpit intended for the same kit. The picture clearly demonstrates that plastic will need to be extensively removed from the plastic kit to enable the resin part to be fitted, which may also need some resin to be removed.

Before chopping parts off a kit to accept resin upgrades, do some planning and measuring. During this process one thing to remember is that the internal measurement of a model aircraft made from injection-moulded plastic cannot be in scale. For example, a commercial airliner skin is approximately 3.175mm thick: scale that down to 1/32 scale and you get 0.0992 – nearly 1/10mm. Some kitchen foil is that thick! Tamiya managed to get cowlings on their 1/32-scale Spitfire down to 0.5mm, which is approaching transparency. Any thinner and the plastic will be brittle and easily damaged.

CUTTING OFF PLASTIC

To apply resin updates to a model will inevitably mean removing plastic sections from the kit. Plan this carefully and mark out the panels that need to be removed. Some panels will be easy, requiring only a cut at each end and scoring along one edge. This can then be lightly broken off. Other panels may require chain drilling or corner holes, and then the use of different-shaped fine razor saws to cut out the centre. To neaten, they will need trimming up with a knife and finishing off with sanding sticks. Rotary saws can be used in an electric drill, but make sure you have speed control otherwise you may cause damage to the kit or to yourself.

The easiest way to remove the panel is to use a razor saw at each end, then score the long engraved line several times with a knife and break the panel off. Finish off all the edges with a sanding stick.

The plastic measured on picking up a random 1/32-scale kit was 1.25mm thick, which when scaled up equals 40mm. This would equate to armoured plate, so there must be some compromise, which is why some cockpits or engines look under scale.

The measurement quoted is from just one manufacturer – others may vary. The problem is compounded when an aftermarket company produces a cockpit which is bigger than the plastic cockpit, as the plastic must then be thinned down to get the cockpit to fit.

A typical set of cutting tools as required to remove panels for resin inserts.

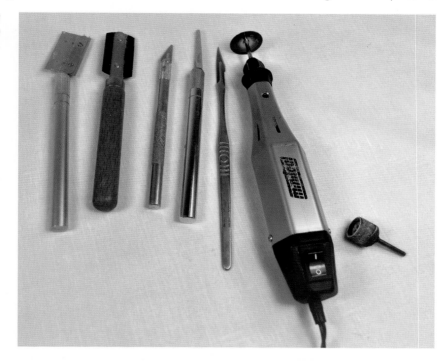

BELOW: *Mark out the panels to be removed with a pencil or marker. Always double check you have the correct panel before cutting.*

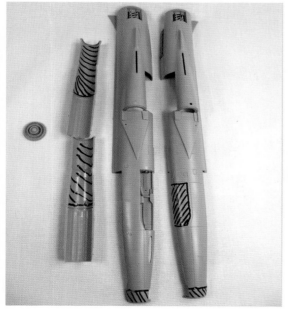

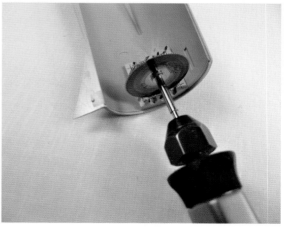

Using a powered cutting disc can cut down the time it takes to remove material, but make a test cut first to make sure you have the right speed. Be aware that if the drill speed is too fast it will melt the plastic, too slow and it may jam up.

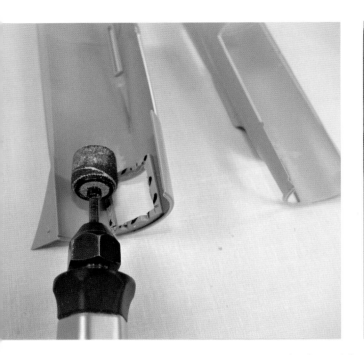
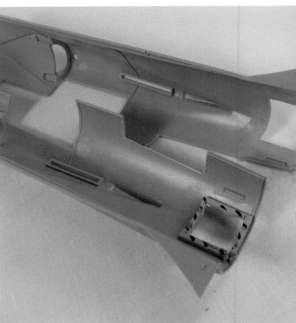

ABOVE LEFT: *Once the four cuts have been made, the middle section can be removed and a drum sanding tool can take away any excess. Again, make sure you keep control of the speed, and take your time.*

ABOVE RIGHT: *One side is complete, but note how thin the rear edge is: this could easily be damaged during cutting and sanding.*

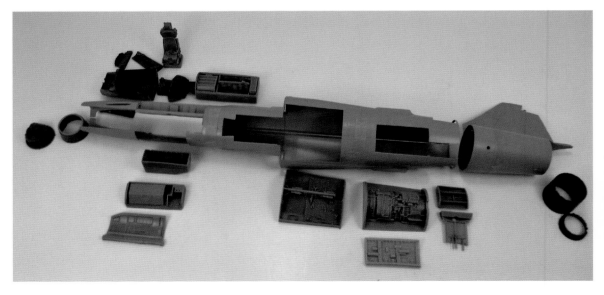

When all the cutting is complete, the fuselage can easily be distorted or damaged, so it is a good idea to tape the two halves together to keep the shape as it should be. Some of the components have been laid out on the bench roughly where they will go. Because this will be a heavy model when it is built, the undercarriage will need to be strong.

COCKPITS

An abundance of optional parts are to be found for cockpits, but you may spend many hours detailing a Hawker Hurricane cockpit in 1/48-scale, which once built and inserted is not visible from outside, whereas a 1/48-scale Tomcat has a massive cockpit and canopy, which can easily be seen from the outside once put together.

This is where the modeller must decide how much he wants to modify the cockpit. For some, it is important to know that every possible bit of detail has been added no matter how much you see, while for others, the available budget may determine how much to put into the model. The advantage to the modeller is that with the most common aircraft, everything from just the seat to a complete cockpit set will be available. The more obscure the aircraft, the more likely it is that the modeller will have to resort to scratch building or using parts from a variety of detail sets.

This 1/48-scale Hawker Hurricane cockpit has been detailed well using a pre-coloured photo etch set, with instrument panel, placards, etched metal seat and seat belts, and even bootstraps on the rudder pedals. When the fuselage is assembled, however, very little of the extensive detail can be seen.

This picture shows that more modern aircraft have much larger cockpits. This 1/48-scale F-14 Tomcat is still a work-in-progress, but it demonstrates that a lot more can be seen on a more modern aircraft, therefore it is worth adding the extra details.

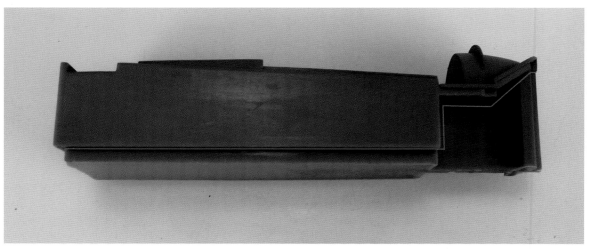

This T-28 Trojan resin cockpit sits to the rear of the centre of gravity. The plastic kit cockpit made the model tail heavy, so it required a nose weight; consequently this resin cockpit will need yet more weight in the nose for it to sit right.

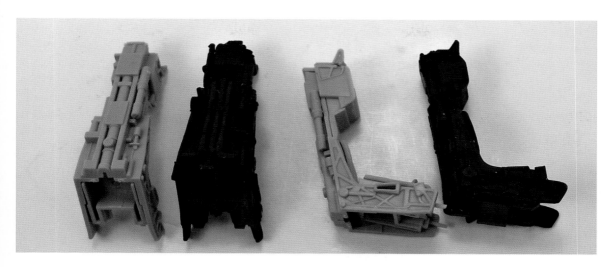

A comparison between injection-moulded seats and resin seats: the seats are from a 1/32-scale Tomcat, and the resin seats are in black primer; the CAD and resin cast seats have far more realistic detail on them, and they usually come with small etch sets of seat belts and placards.

There is a huge range of aftermarket seat sets, and some examples are shown here: on the front row are three 1/48-scale seats – the far one shows a pilot on a modern seat, next is a pilot on a World War II seat, and the third one is a modern seat with belts moulded on. At the back on the left is an early Hawker Hunter seat with all straps moulded on, while the seat on the right represents one from an F-104 Starfighter, with separate accessories and etched brass belts.

Resin cockpits will have excess casting blocks on the cockpit underside. In some cases this can be left on, but this does add to the weight of the model. If the subject has a nose wheel configuration, however, the additional weight may affect the balance of the aircraft, and may cause the aircraft to sit on its tail. Removing the excess is labour-intensive but sometimes necessary. Remove as much as possible, and add weights to the nose area to balance if necessary.

When it comes to detailing seats, injection moulding seems mostly to fail, especially with ejection seats. Many are over or under scale and lack detail. Fortunately, aftermarket companies have stepped up to the mark. All kinds of seats are now produced, from World War I basket-weave seats to the latest ejection seats. Some are produced with seat belts, and some without, and some have seated pilots. Most are available as separate items, and some come in complete cockpit sets.

Instrument panels can be a prominent part of a model aircraft, and there are several ways to do them:

- Paint the plastic kit panel, dry brush any detail and add decal instruments if supplied. If they are not, apply aftermarket decals
- Resin panels can be treated in the same way as described above
- Use a photo-etch panel with negative film. On the back of the film, paint white over the clear

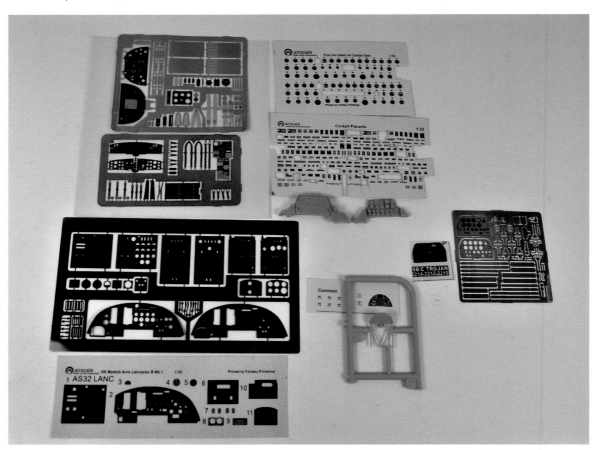

Some different styles of instrument panel, from the very basic, plain, shaped panel with kit-supplied decal, to pre-coloured self-adhesive panels, to a multi-layered etched panel with detailed instrument faces.

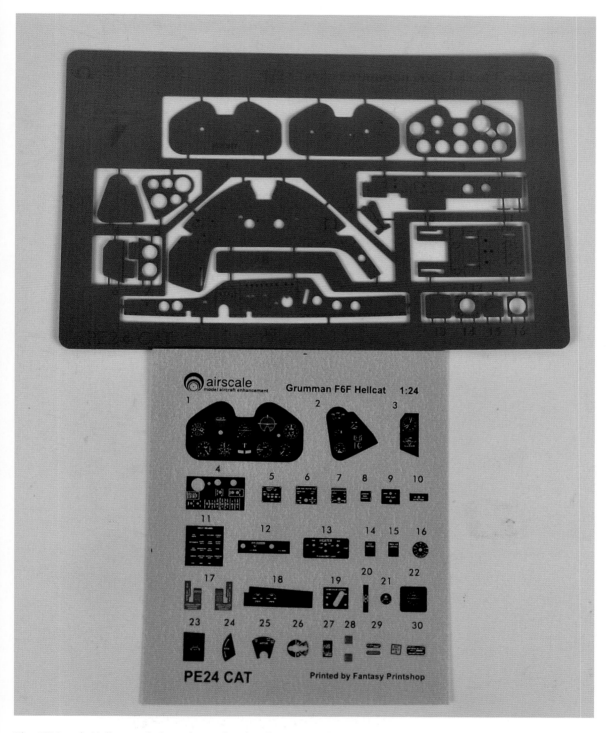

The 1/24-scale Hellcat cockpit set from Airscale. The set incudes side consoles as well as the main instrument panel, which is built up in layers using the back plates, decals, clear acetate film and finally the front panel. The etched brass has been primed ready for the cockpit colours to be applied.

instrument faces. On later aircraft you can add colours and then the white

- Use pre-coloured photo-etch panels. These are built up in layers and can look very effective
- A full cockpit including side panels in photo etch. These will need to be painted first. Back plates are supplied, shaped to the front panels to which the supplied decals are applied, then a clear piece of acetate is sandwiched over the decal simulating glass fronts to the instruments; finally the painted front panel is glued in place.

UNDERCARRIAGE AND WHEEL BAYS

Representing undercarriage bays is an area that has improved over the years. Early injection-moulded bays were often just an empty void, whereas now, with the introduction of CAD-based models, the detail is much better – but there is still room for improvement. Some bays can be improved with the addition of an etched brass set, or the more complex bays with a resin set.

A comparison of the assembled plastic kit parts and the resin replacement. This is a simple undercarriage bay, but still the resin version stands out as having more detail and definition.

The underside of the undercarriage bay showing the resin plugs to be removed. It is possible that more resin will need to be taken off, depending on the space in the wing.

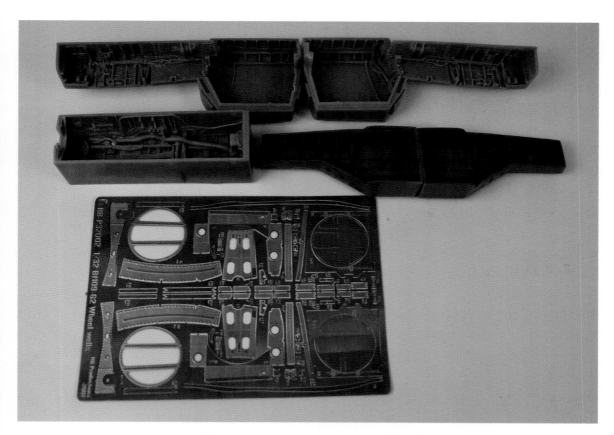

ABOVE: *Samples of resin and etched brass undercarriage bays. The etched brass sheet is for a Bf 109-G2 from RB Productions. The large bays at the back are for a 1/32-scale Tomcat from Aires Hobby Models.*

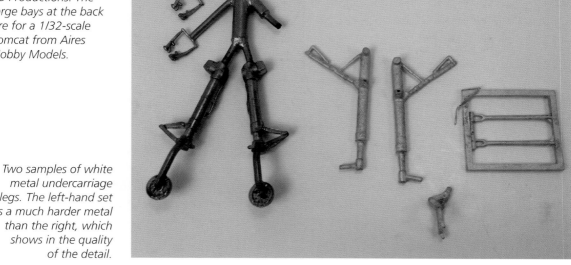

Two samples of white metal undercarriage legs. The left-hand set is a much harder metal than the right, which shows in the quality of the detail.

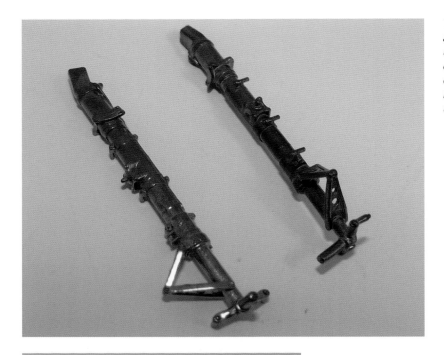

These undercarriage legs are made of bronze and are used in Chapter 8. The model described in Chapter 8 after detailing was 80 per cent resin and etched brass, so the undercarriage had to be strong.

USING A RESIN UNDERCARRIAGE BAY

It is important to note that if a resin under-carriage bay is to be used there is usually a resin casting block that must be removed. In some cases the undercarriage bay is in the wing. This may mean sanding off more than just the casting block, or removing some plastic off the inside wing surfaces. The exact adjustment will depend on the thickness of the plastic and the aerofoil section of the wing. Be careful not to break through into the undercarriage bay when sanding.

Metal undercarriage legs are reproduced for their strength rather than for upgrading detail. Plastic parts are readily broken off accidentally, especially when in transit, for example to exhibitions. Also, if you are adding numerous resin detail sets and etched brass detail sets, weight can be an issue on weak plastic undercarriage legs. Various metals can be used to replace undercarriage legs, from white metal to pewter, brass and bronze. The latter are by far the strongest; white metal can sometimes be too soft and will bend if put under pressure from weight, and the quality of white metal can sometimes be very poor.

FLAPS

There are two main types of flap: aerofoil section and split. Aerofoil flaps will be like a wing, built up with ribs and an outer skin, while split flaps consist of upper and lower halves. The upper part is part of the wing structure, and the lower half hinges from the leading edge of the flap downwards. This is usually built up from ribs and a lower skin. Of all the parts of an aircraft, flaps can be the most awkward to detail. It will normally entail removing a section of the wing and grinding off moulded-on detail on the inside of the upper and lower surface of the wing. Where there is an isolated flap to be removed which is surrounded with plastic that must not be damaged, careful planning is needed to determine where the first cut should be made.

This picture taken at the Cosford RAF Museum shows a split flap partially open. The upper part on some aircraft can be plated in – whether it is depends on how the flap is actuated. The engineering precision shown in the picture also explains why it pays to choose etched brass to replicate these types of flap.

This picture demonstrates the sequence of cuts that need to be made to take out the plastic on an isolated flap. The replacement etched brass flap set includes the complete lower flap section, so the first cut does not have to follow any engraved panel line.

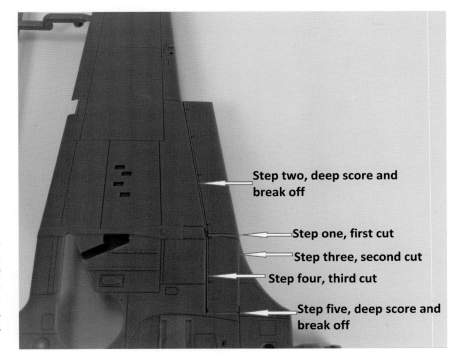

Step two, deep score and break off

Step one, first cut

Step three, second cut

Step four, third cut

Step five, deep score and break off

The upper parts of Hawker Hurricane flap bays are the plated-in type. Note there is a gap between the two plates. This can concern some modellers, but references show that the real aircraft was like this.

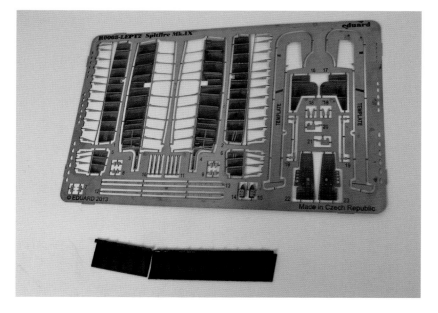

A typical etch set for a 1/48-scale Mk 9 Spitfire, and a built-up set of flaps for a 1/48-scale Hawker Hurricane. The Spitfire set includes templates for setting up the flaps.

When handling etched brass try to make sure your hands are clean, as oils from your skin can mark the etch. Such marks may well interfere with subsequent primers and paint finishes. Before applying paint, clean the etched brass with a small amount of isopropanol.

When removing an aerofoil section flap from a plastic kit, the bottom part is likely to be larger than the top part. This is due to the aerofoil section. Once they have been cut away, the top and bottom parts need to be glued together at the trailing edge. To get an accurate leading edge to the flap it may be necessary to glue a piece of plastic tube or rod to the leading edge. After the glue is dry, fill the voids with a two-pack filler such as Milliput. When this is dry, sand the whole unit to shape. There are, of course, aftermarket resin flaps available for some of the more popular aircraft.

RADIAL ENGINES

Radial engines manufactured in resin by after-market companies can cause a lot of trouble if they are not assembled correctly. The problems usually arise when assembling the cylinders on to the crankcase. Note that some engines have locating devices, as seen in Chapter 8 – but even with these devices designed to aid location, they can still move.

The bases of the cylinders are round, and should fit into round holes on the crankcase. When looking from the front, the cylinders can sometimes be moved left or right, forwards or backwards, and when looking from above can be twisted clockwise or anticlockwise. The level of motion will all depend on how good the fit is in the holes. After cutting off the cylinders from the casting block make sure that the base is square. Use only a slow-drying glue, such as five-minute epoxy glue, to allow you time to adjust the cylinder into the correct position.

Aftermarket resin radial engines are plentiful. This picture shows the same Pratt and Whitney 1830 engine in three different scales: from left to right 1/32 scale, 1/48 scale and 1/72 scale.

A closer view of the 1/72-scale Pratt and Whitney 1830 from Small Stuff. The detail is incredible and could only be done with the use of 3D design and top-quality casting.

The most likely problem to arise when assembling radial engines is shown marked by arrows: the left-hand cylinder is twisted anti-clockwise, and the right-hand cylinder slightly clockwise, and this will interfere with the fitting of intake tubes and push rods.

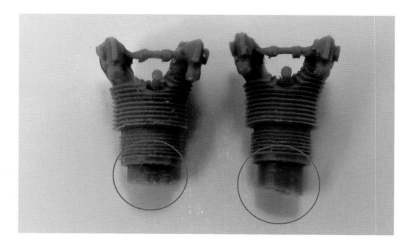

Make sure you cut and trim up the locating stubs squarely and to the same length, once all the cylinders are in place; make sure it fits inside the cowling, if one is being fitted.

ADDITIONAL PARTS IN MULTIMEDIA

Brass Barrels

Other additional parts in multimedia include brass barrels and aluminium turned accessories. One of the major suppliers for these items is Master-Model. Injection-moulded plastic can't produce the definition and crispness of turned metal, and the metal parts are also much stronger. Most of these items are part-for-part replacement for the kit parts. Items such as pitot tubes and some of the larger guns require basic assembly.

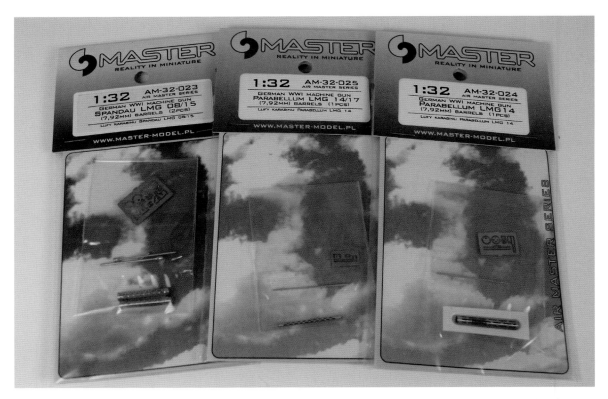

In some World War I plastic kits you may get a small etched brass fret with cooling jackets, which need to be rolled and bonded. This can be a fiddly task, as it can be difficult to get them perfectly round. Master-Model can provide you with accurately milled cooling jackets and barrels. Here is a selection of World War I machine guns.

A selection of World War II machine guns. All are in 1/32 scale, but many of them are also available in the following scales: 1/144, 1/72, 1/48, 1/35, 1/32 and 1/24.

Other items such as refuelling probes, angle of attack probes, and pitot tubes are available. These sets are not too expensive, at around £3 to £5, with gun sets retailing at between £7.50 and £10.

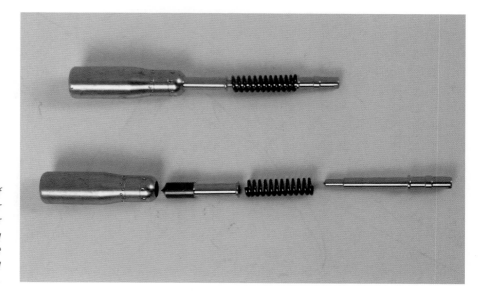

A close-up view of 20mm cannons for the 1/32-scale Hawker Hurricane. The spring is included, and the quality of machining is evident.

Exhausts

Another component that regularly gets replaced is the exhaust. Casting can provide a greater depth to the exhaust outlets. The market holds a wide choice of replacement exhausts for most aircraft kits produced by the many resin companies, and there are some metal versions available.

A company called Moskit was producing metal exhausts that were fully hollow, but unfortunately they did not stay in business; however, another company, Proper Plane from the Ukraine, has discovered the process, and is now manufacturing mostly World War I exhausts in the same manner, together with real laminated-wood propellers.

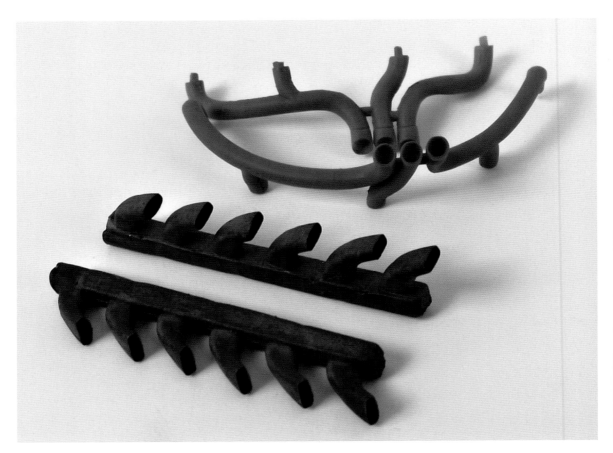

These two resin cast exhausts have a deep recess at the exhaust outlet, which can't be replicated in injection-moulded plastic. The lower two exhausts are from a company called Moskit, and are sadly no longer available, but another company, Proper Plane, are now producing them for World War I aircraft. They are completely hollow and made of very thin metal, and the patina is very realistic, which is especially useful for people who struggle to paint exhaust colours.

Chapter Four

Getting Started with Etched Brass

A good introduction to using etched brass is to make a basic airliner kit. Most mainstream model manufacturers have a range of airliner kits to choose from. Zvezda's 1/144-scale Boeing 767-300 is such a kit: it has no interior detail at all, and the build is a simple one with good fit of parts. Because of the scale, it would be difficult to represent in etch a level of detail for the interior, which would be visible. The only etch pieces used are three vent panels, engine fan discs, pitot heads

ZVEZDA 1/144-SCALE BOEING 767-30

Detail set used:
- Metallic Details MD14414 (etched brass)
- Flying Colors FC44-039R Hawaiian Airlines (decals)

- Flying Colors FC44-052 Coroguard Decals (decals)

References used: Google Search Hawaiian Airlines images.

The finished model of Hawaiian Airlines 767-300ER. Colourful schemes such as these make attractive desktop models.

(continued)

Zvezda 1/144-Scale Boeing 767-30 *(continued)*

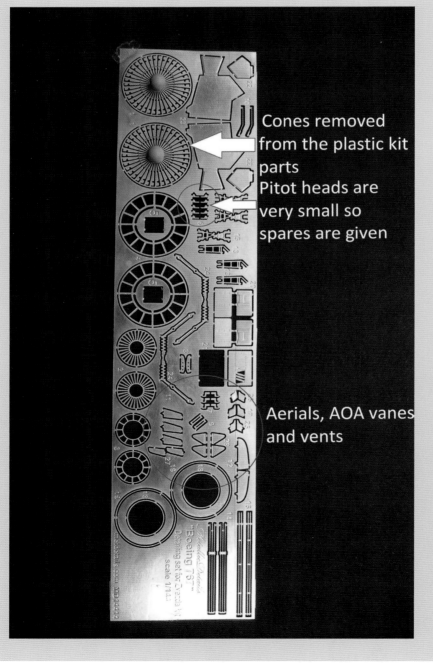

The Metallic Details etch set used in this project. Not all the details will be used, as the aircraft will be displayed in flight.

Cones removed from the plastic kit parts

Pitot heads are very small so spares are given

Aerials, AOA vanes and vents

and aerials. This kit helps the modeller make a simple start in using etched brass, but the small details provided can make a big difference to the finished effect.

Before starting work on your model, it is worth spending time thinking about how you want the final piece to look, and how best to show the additional detailing you have applied. How to display aircraft model is very much a personal choice. In the author's opinion, airliner models usually look better on a stand in flight mode, rather than on their undercarriage on the ground, and consequently the build demonstrated took this into account. There are some model airliners in larger scales, such as the 1/125-scale Airbus A380 or 1/72-scale 737-200 with additional detailing, which look very good when displayed on undercarriage.

MAKING THE ZVEZDA 1/144-SCALE BOEING 767-300

A quick look through the instructions for the etched brass kit shows that most of the set deals

with the undercarriage and engines, with one vent panel designed to be cut into the fuselage, and two vents, one on each engine. The three vents were dealt with first by chain drilling the areas that needed to be opened, then using a sharp pointed knife and files to neaten up all the edges. When folding the vents to be fitted, a curve needed adding to ensure they sat flush with the curves of the fuselage and engine cones. A small amount of filler can be added as necessary to make sure the surfaces all blend together well.

The kit comes with strips of windows that were fitted from the inside of the fuselage, before assembling the fuselage halves together. The nose undercarriage bay was glued into place, even though the intended display was of the model in flight mode, as the nose gear doors sit on its edge.

While the fuselage was drying, the engines were assembled using the etched parts from the Metallic Details set. Their instructions were studied carefully, as there is only a basic diagram to work with. The plastic engines have two pieces that needed parts cut off, the bullet nose from the intake fan (part C14) and the rear cone parts C26, which needed to have the rear plastic blades

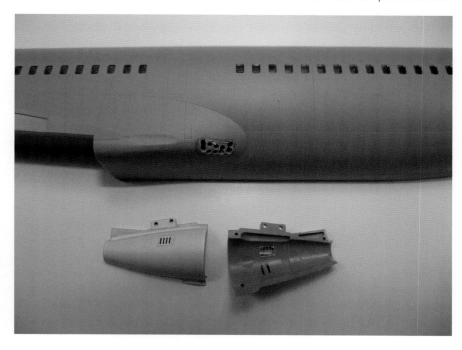

Work on the fuselage and engine vents under way. Thick plastic is best chain drilled on larger vents, while smaller vents can be done by drilling one hole and finishing off with a sharp knife and a file.

This fuselage vent was in an awkward place, as it was on a curved fairing. It means the brass insert needed to be curved to match. Inevitably filling was needed around the edge of the panel for a smooth mating of the two surfaces.

removed. A thin, fine-cut razor saw was used with care, as the bullet nose on C14 was required for later in the build, whereas the forward disc part to C26 was discarded.

Fine-point tweezers were used to twist the forward intake fan blades to an angle. Once this was completed, the designed two rings were placed into the slots on the blades. The two rings are very delicate and require careful cutting and placement, but the overall effect is very good. They are fragile so were worked slowly, and dry fitted carefully because if the fan or turbine blades are too big when the engine is put together it will crush them. The fit of the engine parts with this kit was not problematic. The next stage was to assemble the wings and tail planes and glue the wings into place, but the tail planes needed to be placed to one side until the decals for the rear fuselage were in place.

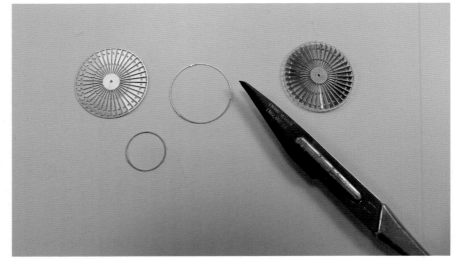

The plastic kit supplies the modeller with solid plastic fan blades. On the real aircraft it is possible to see through these to the rear turbine blades. Etched brass fan blades are a much better way to represent this.

The rear turbine blades are also represented in the etch set, which adds to the overall effect, especially when viewed from the front.

BELOW: *All the major assemblies have been completed and the basic paint scheme applied. The next step is to apply gloss clear coat to accept the Hawaiian decal scheme.*

The exterior paintwork on this aircraft, like many commercial aircraft, is basic. It consists of white fuselage, grey wings with polished leading edges to fin, tail planes, engine intake ring and the main planes. The visually satisfying part comes with the colourful Hawaiian scheme. Once the basic scheme had been applied, the Flying Colors decals were applied around the tail. There were three main parts to each side, which would have been more easily applied had they been broken down into more pieces. The large decals that went around compound curves needed a fair amount

of trimming, plus many applications of decal softener to iron out the wrinkles.

Once the main scheme and stencils were applied, the engines and tail planes were glued into place, and the aircraft was glued to its stand. The final parts to be applied – which make a difference to small-scale airliners – are the pitot tubes, AOA vanes, aerials and vents fitted around the fuselage. A small 0.3mm hole was drilled at each location to accept and aid the bonding, then a small amount of medium superglue was placed in the hole and the part placed into it.

The model has all the Hawaiian decals on, including stencils. The model needed another coat of gloss clear to seal everything in, and was then set to one side to cure fully. When cured, the tail planes and engines were attached and the model glued to its stand.

Final touches are now in place: blade aerials, pitot heads and AOA vanes. These items are all very small (the pitot and AOA vanes being approximately 1.5mm in length).

GETTING STARTED WITH ETCHED BRASS/NICKEL SILVER

The kit used for this project was the Tamiya 1/48-scale Spitfire Mark 1, one of the latest 1/48-scale kits to come from Tamiya. This sort of kit presentation is becoming more common now: everything the modeller requires to achieve a high standard of detail is in the box, thereby eliminating the need to pay more to get extra details. The company revisited their original boxing of the Mark 1 Spitfire, correcting some shape issues and updating the kit with all-new tooling. The updated kit includes a nickel-silver etch fret containing thirty parts. Other changes include alternative parts for an open or a closed canopy, the choice of an open or a closed cockpit door, alternative cockpit parts for early Mark 1 Spitfires, paint masks for the canopy, and markings for three different aircraft.

The only tools required for the nickel-silver etch fret are a sharp knife, flat-nosed tweezers or smooth-faced box-nosed pliers. All the folding is designed to be done with small location tabs, making this an easy kit to start photo-etch assembly.

Fuselage Assembly

This build was strictly out of the box, and only parts supplied in the kit were used. The assembly begins with deciding what final scheme is desired, and whether to have the canopy open or closed. These decisions need to be made at the beginning, before building begins, because as you progress through the instructions they indicate where alternative parts are to be fitted for the different versions. Approximately half of the etched parts are for use in the cockpit area, and the rest are designed for use externally on the wings and

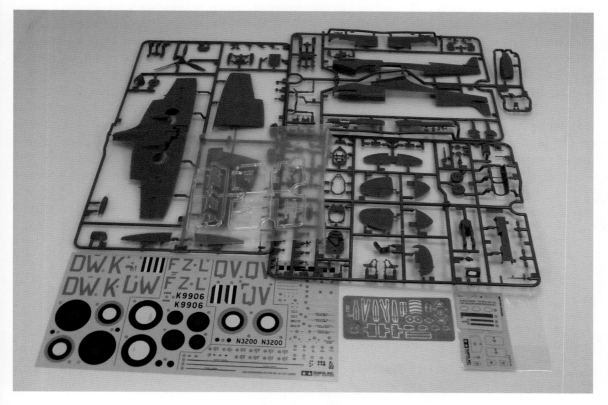

This parts layout of the Tamiya Mark 1 kit shows just how complete the kit is. It includes options such as canopy masks, nickel-silver etched sheet, and three choices of markings.

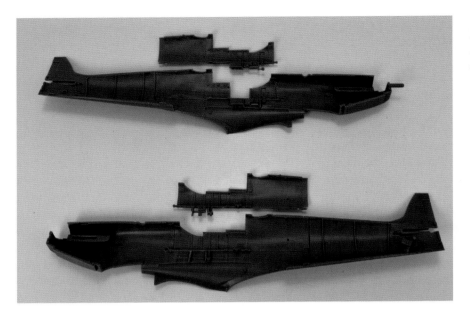

The option of illustrating a closed canopy and a shut side door can be seen here. The open canopy option is glued into place, with the optional parts shown above the fuselages.

fuselage. Not all the etched parts were used in this build.

Once the decision was made regarding which version was to be made, the cockpit walls were glued to the fuselage sides and primed. Many of the small parts for the cockpit were also primed and painted before they were removed from the sprues. The instrument panel was painted black, and the instruments represented from the decals on the sheet provided. For this scale the represented panel looks very effective.

The use of photo etch does not start until section five of the build, with the initial parts being bootstraps for the rudder pedals, seat straps, compass bracket, and the frame top for part A9. Some nickel-silver seatbelts can be hard and thick, making them springy and difficult to bend into shape, and so requiring annealing, but these from Tamiya are thin and easy to conform to shape without having to anneal them.

As with any build, dry fit any assemblies as you go along to ensure accuracy and to allow for any corrections. This Tamiya kit had an excellent fit so there was no need for any adjustments. The cockpit assembly was glued into place and the fuselage halves were closed and held together while applying Tamiya extra-thin cement. If you use masking tape to ensure the joints do not come

The first etched parts to be fitted are the rudder pedal bootstraps and the compass bracket. The compass bracket is made by simply folding up the two sides, and the bootstraps were folded around a drill-bit shank.

All the interior sub-assemblies are ready to be assembled together and installed.

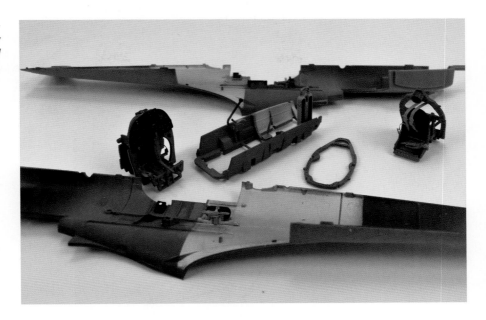

apart, be careful that capillary action does not creep under the masking tape. If it does, it will leave glue marks that will require sanding when dry, putting you to unnecessary effort.

While the glue dried, the tail planes and elevators were assembled along with the undercarriage bays, and other small sub-assemblies required for the wings. Positioning and gluing the tailplanes was straightforward, and once fitted, the small elevator attachment cover provided on the etch fret (part A10) was folded and fitted. It was important to note the arrows engraved on this part, which indicate the correct orientation. Following this, the rudder and tail-wheel assembly was fitted.

An error was made when painting the cockpit parts. Spitfire seats were usually composite material

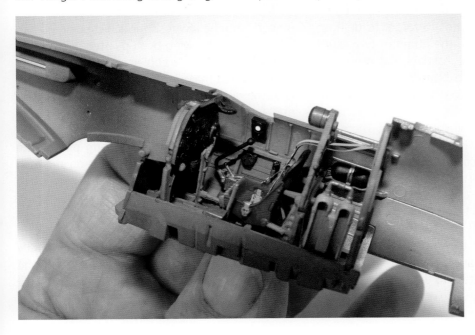

Dry fitting the cockpit is essential. If possible, also put the second side fuselage in place to make sure all is going to fit together correctly, and then make any adjustments necessary.

The arrow indicates where the etched elevator access plate A-10 is fitted. Note the etched arrow indicator on the inside surface.

painted a reddish-brown colour, but early Spitfires had aluminium seats painted in interior green. The purpose of this story is to encourage modellers to 'read the instructions', which correctly indicate that the seat interior should be painted green.

Wing Assembly

The wing assembly starts with the installation of the undercarriage bays and four outer gun-barrel ends. It was important not to forget to drill out the four holes to enable the fitting of two external air vents later. Once installed, the wing tops were glued to the wing bottom, and once this was dry the wing tips and ailerons were fitted. The next etched parts to be fitted were associated with the radiator and oil cooler faces. These are very straightforward, with only a tab to bend to enable it to fit into a corresponding locating slot, which has a raised part on the plastic part on to which it bonds.

The plastic part A41 was painted black, then the etch front and back grills were painted a dark metallic colour, so as to give a contrast to the black. These were made up as sub-assemblies, but not immediately fitted to the wing. When the wings were ready, they were dry fitted to the fuselage, and when all lined up well the wings were

glued to the fuselage. On this kit all the joints were perfect, and no filler was required at all.

Tamiya have also approached the undercarriage system very well. Both legs are attached to a bar, which is inserted into the wing, thus setting the undercarriage to the correct angles. The bar is then covered with plates, which simulate actual plates on the real aircraft, again with perfect joins so that no filler is required. At this stage the aircraft was primed, and the lower surfaces were painted aluminium. Had the wing been painted after gluing on the radiator and oil cooler, it would risk getting paint on areas that would be problematic to cover with the radiator fitted, so painting first saves on masking later.

The final pieces of etch fitted were the ring and bead sight plus the two reinforcing plates. The reinforcing plates are manufactured on the etch set and a self-adhesive sheet. They are designed to go along the bottom edge of the fuel-tank cover. Looking at references of Mark 1 Spitfires showed that the prototype had them fitted, but they were not evident on aircraft in service – consequently the decision was made to leave them off the model, because in 1/48 scale they would possibly be represented at overscale.

Undercarriage bays assembled and fitted; the centre part helps to keep the dihedral of the wings. When dry, the wing tops, ailerons and wing tips can be fitted, glued and set aside to dry.

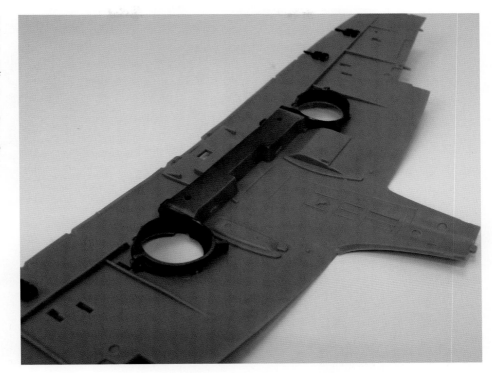

Note that the area circled needs to be painted aluminium, as it can be seen under the rear cockpit floor.

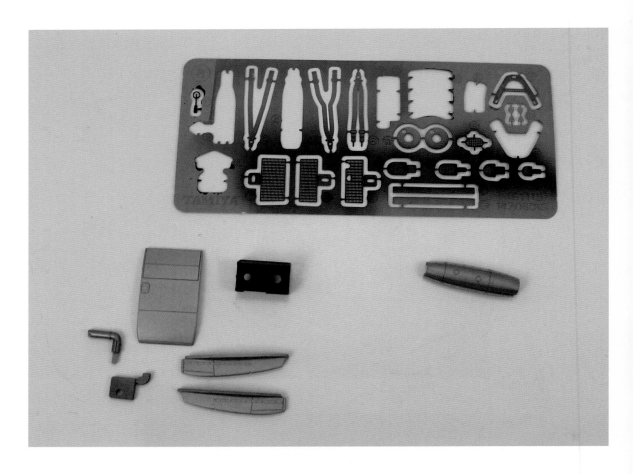

ABOVE: *The oil cooler and radiator assemblies with the etch set. Be aware there are spare parts on the etch set for possible later variants, so be sure to use the correctly numbered parts.*

Tamiya's engineers came up with a very clever way of getting the undercarriage to the correct splay and angle. They are moulded in one piece with a bar between them, which is inserted into the wing. Plates then cover the bar leaving no gaps so that everything is strong.

ABOVE: *All the lower surfaces were painted aluminium after priming, including the radiator and oil cooler sub-assemblies. Doing this enables you to paint areas that would be difficult to get to were they fully assembled in place.*

The unused reinforcing plates are on the etch set, though not mentioned in the instructions, as is the self-adhesive sheet, which is mentioned. It requires some cutting out, removing the self-adhesive glue, and then gluing on to the airframe with craft glue.

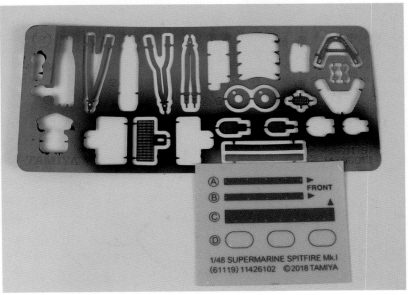

After the main assembly had been completed the cockpit was masked off using soft sponge, then camouflage was applied and given a coat of gloss clear, ready to accept decals.

The finished aircraft upper surfaces.

The finished aircraft lower surfaces.

All the final small parts such as wheels, undercarriage doors, pitot head and canopy were painted separately. The cockpit and lower surfaces were masked off with sponge pieces and masking tape, and the camouflage applied. After a coat of gloss varnish, all the stencils and markings were applied, followed by a clear matt finish. The final touch was to attach a fine wire from the rudder post to the aerial mast. This was a simple introduction to using etched brass, but with careful preparation and assembly a well-detailed rendition of a Mark 1 Spitfire was achieved, making the kit suitable for any level of model making, even by a beginner. Tamiya have a reputation of quality kits, and this one is no exception.

Chapter Five

Adding Multimedia Details

The Italeri 1/48-scale Westland Wessex has been released in three variants: HAS 1, HAS 3, and the HU 5. The kit has etched brass parts supplied that cover some grilles around the tail unit, the instrument panel, the large grille covering the main rotor gear box, the cockpit roof plate, and some seatbelts for the cockpit. Only a few of these items will be used, but they are all useful to have as spares in case of accidents.

The Italeri kit parts assemble very well, but the drawback to these kits is the rear cabin. This is left empty except for the HU 5, which has some troop seats supplied. The HAS 3 should have a large sonar housing and control panel for two operators on the port side, and a spare seat on the starboard side. The HAS 31b Australian version can be built from the original kit with a few simple additions: the Scalewarship Ltd main rotor fold and

The finished kit assembled as HMS Antrim's *ship's flight* circa 1977. *HMS* Antrim *was guard ship to the Queen on her Silver Jubilee tour of the Caribbean.*

THE 1/48-SCALE ITALERI WESTLAND WESSEX HAS 3

The kit used for the build in this chapter is the 1/48-scale Italeri Westland Wessex HAS 3, together with extra details, resin, 3D prints and photo etch.
The following detail sets were used:

• Rotor Craft tail fold set RC-4809 (resin)
• Eduard interior set 49-622 (etched brass)
• Scalewarship rotor fold set (3D prints and etched brass)

• Hannants Xtradecal set X48111 (decals)
• INFINI model flight-deck tie-down points (etched brass)

The following references were used:

• Warpaint series No. 65 Westland Wessex
• 4+ publication Westland Wessex
• http://www.britmodeller.com/forums/index.php?/forum/341-rotary-wing-aircraft-walkarounds/

Italeri Westland Wessex HAS 3 box art.

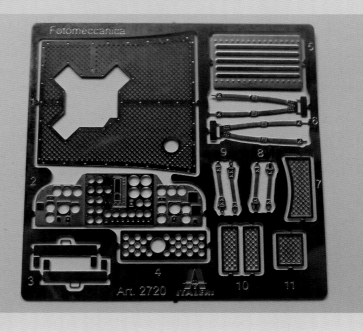

The etched brass set supplied with the kit can be used in conjunction with the Eduard and Rotorcrafts tail fold set. They can be mixed and matched as required.

The author's first Italeri Wessex build as an Australian HAS 31b; the experience of building some of the etched brass parts for this model helped with the build of the HAS 3 kit.

the Southern Sky Models Royal Australian Navy decals.

It was decided to use the HAS 3 version and make it into a ship's flight from HMS *Antrim*. For this model the main cabin door is shown closed, the tail unit and main rotor blades folded, and the aircraft is tied down to a deck section as if ready to be put into the on-board hangar. The main areas of additional detailing are therefore the cockpit, tail fold and main rotor fold.

STARTING ASSEMBLY

Before tackling any extra detailing, check over the chosen kit for short shot areas, warping or damage. It is well worth spending a few days or even weeks studying the kit and all the accessories purchased for the build, also gathering and studying references, and planning out the stages in which you propose to proceed. There will be several different instruction sheets with

which to become familiar. A practice worth adopting is to check through the etched brass instructions first, then to mark the kit instruction sheet at the point where the etched brass is to be used.

When checking over the parts it is worth taking some measurements of both the kit and of resin parts to make sure the resin parts will fit. Take a measurement on any curved surface of the maximum width and height where a cut is to be made to insert a resin component, and compare this with the resin replacement.

The instructions for the tail fold suggest removing the tail-wheel assembly and then making one straight cut to remove the tail area. However, always leave a little plastic to sand back to the line marked. You can easily sand a little more, but it's not that easy to add material back on if you go too far. On the model depicted, the cut was taken around the tail-wheel assembly. This preserved the plate where the tail wheel met the fuselage.

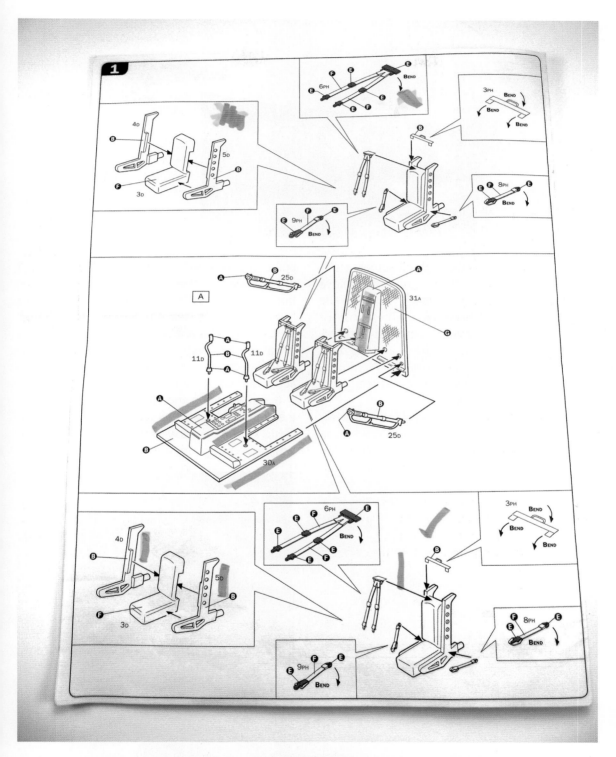

Marking the instruction sheets with a marker pen where etched brass is to be introduced or changed with kit parts helps with the method of construction.

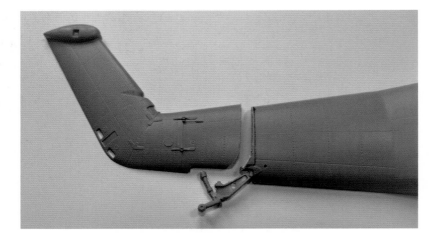

Decision time: once you have made the cut, you are committed. Always leave a little plastic that you can sand back to – this is far more controlled than it would be to cut to the line.

As with most aircraft kits, the assembly starts with the cockpit. One of the first jobs is to remove detail from the plastic parts, ready to receive the pre-coloured etched brass parts. These consist of the instrument panel, between-the-seats console with the throttle quadrant, and the overhead panel. Once the detail has been removed, the main cockpit bulkhead, floor and rear cabin assembly can be put together.

As with most etched brass detail sets, not every component from the set needs to be used – you can mix and match to suit. With the illustrated build, one seat was made up entirely of etched brass, while the other utilized the plastic cushions from the kit with the etched brass seat frames from the Eduard set. On this second seat Mr Surfacer 500 was applied, and while it was drying it was stippled with a stiff-haired brush to simulate a sheepskin surface. A similar effect can be accomplished by using a modelling putty.

If you are using the etched brass seat frames, there are four holes that require filling where the plastic kit seat frames were to be fitted. You can use a spare piece of plastic rod, or filler, for the purpose.

Detailed plastic parts that need to be sanded back if it is intended to use the coloured photo etch from the Eduard set. Some of the parts are duplicated in the illustration for comparison between those as moulded and those prepared.

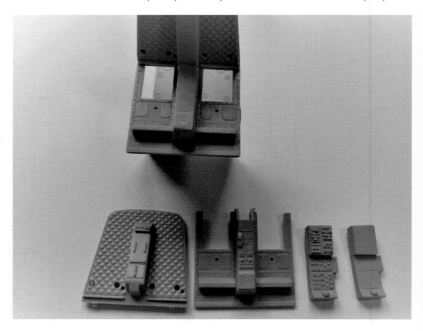

The two ways you can use photo etch are demonstrated here. One seat has been built fully from etched brass, the other one has been built using the etched brass framework with the plastic seat cushions from the kit.

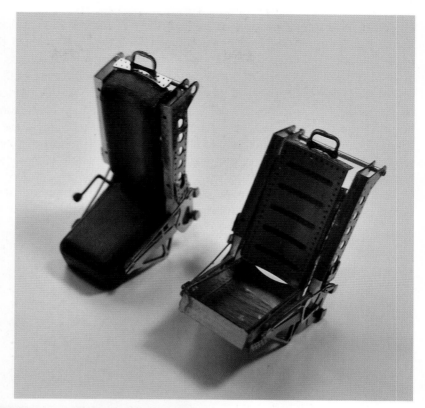

The assembled basic cockpit and rear cabin. Note the plastic rod used for blocking off the holes meant for the plastic seat frames.

Once the main cabin assembly has dried, it is worth doing some dry fitting. Experience with the Australian HAS 31b shows that the cockpit side walls in the Eduard set interfere with the main cockpit assembly, as the tolerances are very tight.

Some of this is due to the way the etched brass side walls are folded up. Eduard produce them in one piece, instructing you to fold the top rail over and then fold up the ribs to fit under the rail. This leaves four protrusions under the bottom edge.

These will need filing down so they are flush with the back plate. Alternatively you can remove the ribs entirely and glue them on separately.

In addition to this there is a raised bar on each side of the plastic cockpit floor that can be sanded down, as well as a locating strip close to the bottom surface, which needs to be removed from the starboard side of the fuselage. After making these alterations, the cockpit assembly and the brass side walls will fit perfectly.

At this stage some small bare brass components need to be assembled: control boxes, levers, and console side plates. After gluing them in place they will need to be primed and painted using the interior colours, before applying the coloured etched brass panels.

Finally, the rear cabin windows will need to be fitted, and before installing the cockpit and cabin assembly, there are some flashed-over holes that must be opened and inserts put in place on the fuselage sides from the inside. Be careful here as there are different holes for different marks of aircraft that utilize the same rear fuselage sides.

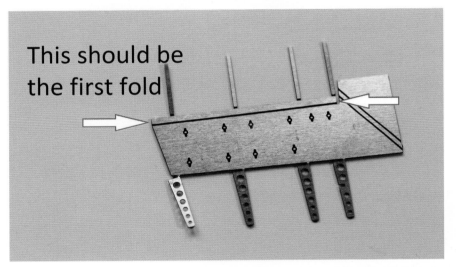

Folds in etched brass need to be made in the right sequence.

A 'hold and fold' tool is best used on small, narrow folds.

All the other folds on this piece are easily completed using tweezers. Fold up the ribs and tack in place, then fold down the top strip on to the rib and tack in place.

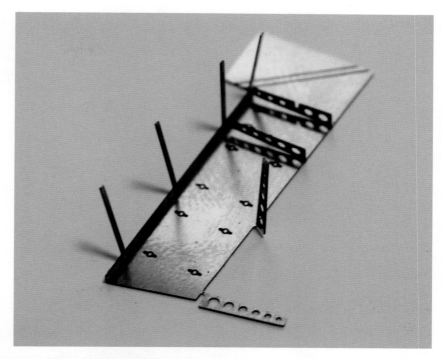

BELOW: *The finished side walls. The left side has been primed for clarity.*

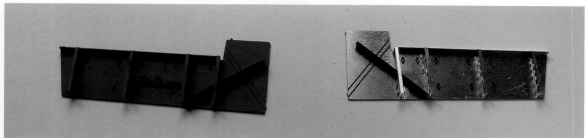

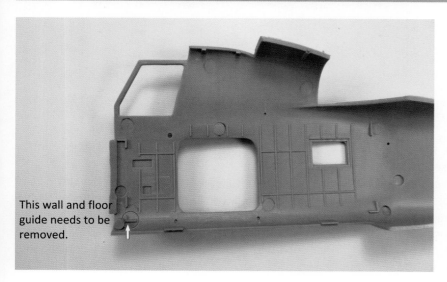

This wall and floor guide needs to be removed.

When using the etched brass cockpit side walls, some minor adjustments may be required. This picture shows one area that seems to be a problem, because left in place, it lifts the cockpit floor too high. By removing this locator, and also the raised plastic strip on the edge of the cockpit floor, the etch side walls should be a snug fit and at the right height.

To ensure the etch side walls will fit, the strips on the edge of the cockpit have been sanded back, and some of the etched brass fittings have been put in place.

Some of the etched brass fittings are very small, as demonstrated by comparison with this penny. Most of the folds were made using flat-nosed tweezers or box-nosed pliers.

The next stage is to glue the cabin assembly in place and assemble the fuselage halves together. Once this is dry the bottom of the fuselage can be glued in place. The nose assembly, including the instrument panel and coaming, can be assembled while the fuselage is drying. Once the fuselage has dried, the nose section can be glued in place. Note there is one hole that needs opening for the bracket that supports the bonnet (part number 23b).

Turning to the tail section, the forward part of the two-part resin tail fold will need to be slightly adjusted at the bottom edge, as will the inside surface of the fuselage. Once the fit of the adjoining parts is satisfactory, they will require bonding into place with five-minute epoxy glue or with a slow-

Two starboard fuselage halves showing before and after the opening of holes and fitting of blanks. This must be completed before the cockpit and cabin is fitted.

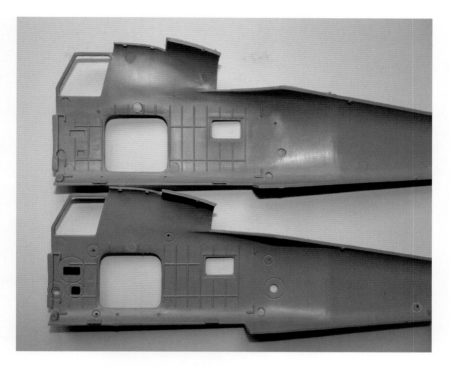

setting superglue. This provides the time to further adjust the fit, and then any minor filling of any gaps can be completed. The rear part (tail fin) of the conversion will require the etched parts to be attached from the small set supplied, which are mostly grilles.

There are always other areas of extra detailing that can be carried out in the cockpit for those who want to add extra finesse, but for this subject and scale what has been described looks busy enough for the overall effect required.

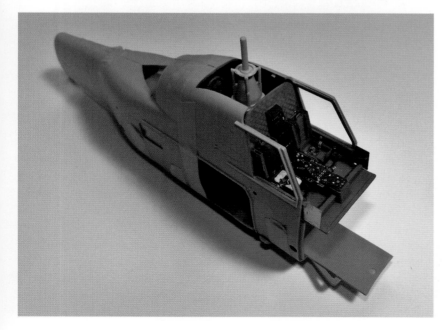

The fuselage halves have been glued together, including the bottom panel. All are being held together with tape to ensure a good bond.

Dry fitting the nose. The illustration shows that even after putting in extras to the cockpit, the fit is a good one. This will be glued and held in place with some tape.

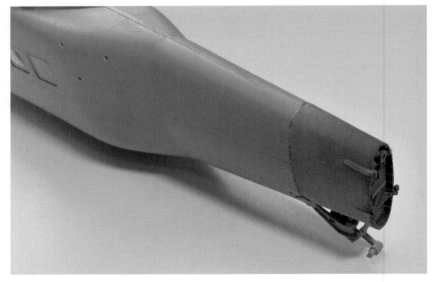

After ensuring everything fitted well, the first part of the resin tail fold was glued in place using five-minute epoxy glue. This gave time to adjust the part before the glue set.

In section seven of the instructions, the nose section is glued in place along with the exhausts, the oil cooler outlet fairing and other small details. This is where it is necessary to consider the colour scheme. On the illustrated subject it is the late 1970s yellow and blue/grey scheme. The dividing line, especially around the fuselage sides and cockpit, coincides with many pipes, fairings and undercarriage struts, which are the next items to be fitted according to the instructions. With this

scheme, however, these are better left until after the main paint scheme is complete. This means moving around the instructions between sections eight, nine and ten, and fitting only the major components that will not interfere with the paint scheme. If the choice of paint scheme is one solid colour, then these awkward fittings can be glued on as instructed, and the paint scheme applied.

In the illustrated build, black Ultimate primer was applied to the cockpit frames first, followed with white Ultimate primer over all the major components. Having a white base helps to bring out the yellow and blue-grey colours. Both colours were applied using Hannants Xtracolour range of enamel paints. These dried to a glossy finish, eliminating any need to apply a clear coat for decal application.

After the markings were applied, they were then sealed in with two coats of Alclad II aqua gloss. This toned down the gloss levels for a more realistic look. While the clear coat was drying, all the small components, fairings, undercarriage struts, wheels, aerials and so on were painted and prepared for fitting.

One detail that must be considered is the curve in the main rotor blades. Italeri moulded the blades with the correct curve to them for unfolded blades. When the blades are folded, they are very nearly straight. There are two methods to adjust the moulded blades to get the right effect: either the blades can be immersed in hot water then clamped between wood blocks, or by holding the blade at the root with one hand, they can be pulled

through between the thumb and forefinger of the other hand, bending in the opposite direction from the moulded curve. Experience with both methods suggests that the latter method is more effective.

Before assembling the main rotor head, the moulded rotor fold attached to the blade will need to be cut in two places with a fine-cut razor saw. Having made the cuts, the three-dimensional parts can be removed from the sprue, and the part attached to the blade can be glued into place. It is important to ensure the correct orientation of the fold. A small amount of superglue can be used as a filler to blend in the blade fold to the blade.

The rotor head can now be assembled, including the plastic part previously cut off. This will need to have a 1mm hole drilled into its centre to accept the second three-dimensional part, but it should not be glued until later. All four of the blade folds are at different angles, so this piece will need to be rotated to achieve the correct angle. Once the main rotor fold and tail rotor assembly have been assembled and painted, they can be put to one side until final assembly.

All the main components have been glued in place, and all the etched brass grilles have been fitted prior to priming.

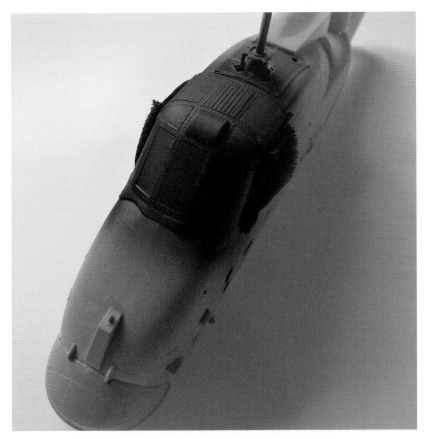

After masking off the cockpit and cabin windows, matt black primer was applied to the canopy frames. The frames will therefore be the correct colour when looking into the cockpit.

BELOW: White primer applied over all the airframe will provide a good base on to which to spray the yellow. If any rubbing down on the yellow areas is necessary, it is important to ensure there is no breakthrough to the primer. Yellow pigment is weak, so any dark spots will be difficult to cover.

Once the yellow was applied and dry, the demarcation lines were marked out. Care is needed to make sure the line around the cockpit and nose is level when viewed from both the side and the front.

The main colour scheme is complete, and the markings and stencils have been applied.

Finally, assemble the Scalewarship saddle and blade holders according to the instructions. The blade holders are best folded around the rotor blade itself, and the small brackets attached. The saddle, once assembled, can be placed on to the model.

The next stage is to fit all the small ancillaries from sections eight to fourteen that were not fitted earlier, and to touch up any paintwork as necessary. Rotor Craft's instructions do not say how to fit the tail section in the folded position, and there are only two small hinge points to which to attach it. On real aircraft there is a small latch protruding out of the fuselage which latches on to the hand-hold on the trailing edge of the tail. A replica of this could be applied to the model, but on this model, drilling a 0.5mm hole from the top hinge point on both resin sections and inserting a piece of brass rod will add considerable strength. Superglue added on the two hinge points and the brass rod will hold the tail section well.

The final assembly is the tail rotor, main rotor blades and hub fitting. The main rotor hub needs to be placed but not glued into the gearbox assembly. Starting with the innermost blades, one of the blade holders slides on to the blade roughly in the correct position, the second 3D printed part meshes on to the blade end part, in an open position.

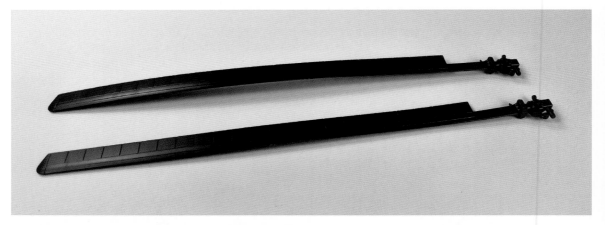

The main rotor blades are moulded with the correct curve in them for extended blades. These will need to be straightened like the lower one for a demonstration of folded blades.

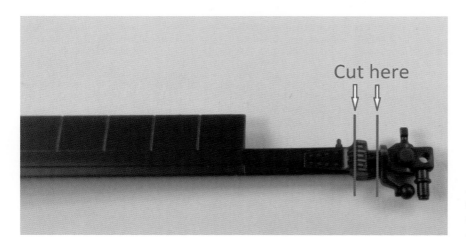

Shown here are the two cuts that need to be made for attaching the 3D parts.

The 3D printed parts. The left-hand part does not need to have a pin, but part of it can be saved and used if desired. The right-hand part needs the use of the pin, so the cut is made where indicated by the arrow.

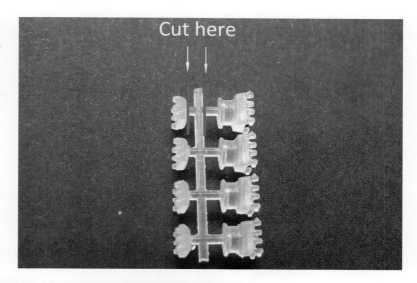

All the parts are assembled, but the four knuckle joints that go on to the rotor head are not glued until final assembly.

Folding and assembling the blade holders is best completed on the blade to give a snug fit, and for ease of handling. Be careful not to accidently glue the holder to the blade.

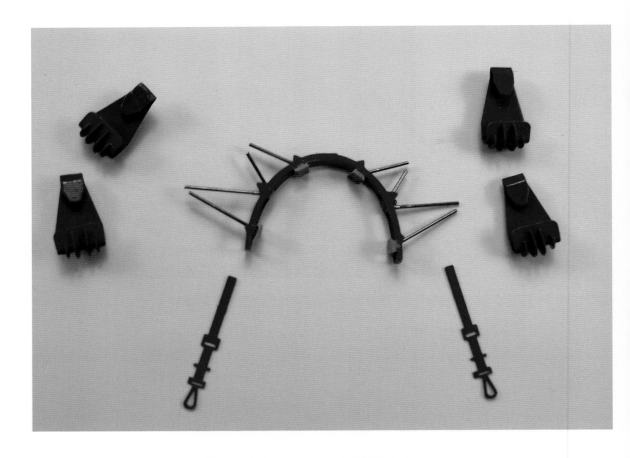

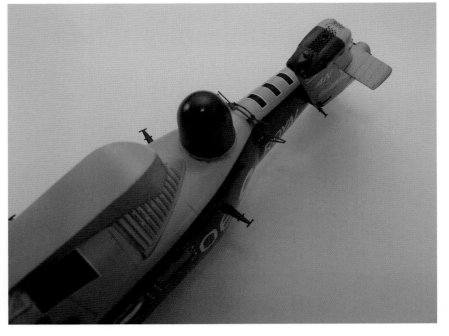

ABOVE: *Assembling the rods to the saddle at the right angle is very fiddly. Only a small amount of glue should be used here; alternatively a flexible glue can be used so that adjustments can be made when fitting the blades and blade holders.*

Small plastic card pads have been added to the underside of the saddle and then fitted to the airframe.

The next part is fiddly. The 3D printed part is offered into the previously drilled hole on the rotor head assembly, and at the same time the blade holder is aligned to the rods on the saddle. Once the two inner blades are in position, everything is more stable. The same process is carried out on the outer two blades.

Finally, the tail rotor can be fitted, and if desired the blade holder and rods for the tail rotor can be scratch built. These attach to the saddle but are not supplied in the Scalewarship set.

Some final details, such as aerials, exhausts and wiper blades, are fitted before attaching to the base. The exhausts in the kit look to be under scale, so thin-walled aluminium tube can be substituted after applying some Alclad II burnt metal to the exhaust bases.

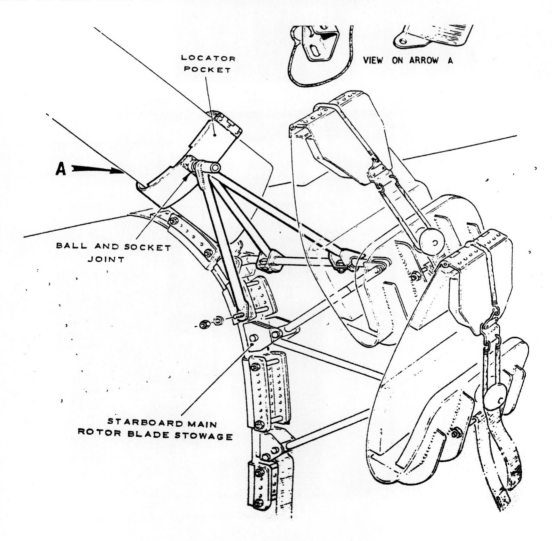

Maintenance manuals are a good source of information. Some manuals are available from companies online or from museum archives. Finding a photo of the tail rotor attachment to the main saddle was not possible, so the Westland Wessex maintenance manual was a very useful alternative source of information.

The whole assembly in place. Getting to this stage requires patience and dexterity as assembly of the small components is fiddly, but it is well worth the effort as the representation looks 'the part'.

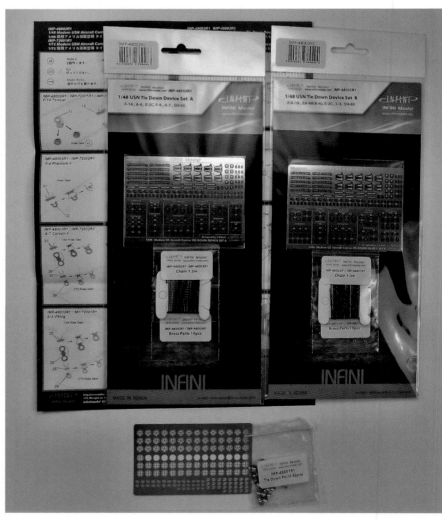

The INFINI tie-down sets are good value as they contain many parts within each set.

The flight-deck base comes with a simulated textured surface, which can be lightly rubbed down and painted dark grey. The tie-down sets are available from a company called INFINI Model. These sets are meant for modern United States Navy carrier decks, but many of the parts are universal. The detail is incredibly small, so patience is required to build up the parts, but when complete the tie-down points look more realistic. The straps can be made from masking tape or lead foil.

The parts required to make up one tie-down strap give incredibly fine detail and require patience to assemble.

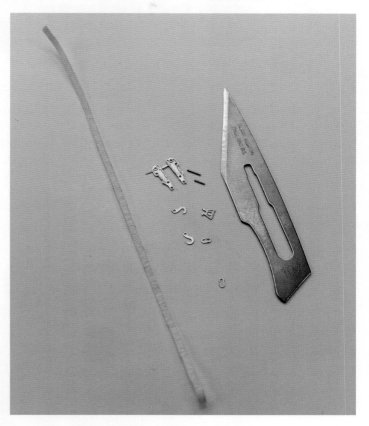

BELOW: *The finished Westland Wessex project on a flight-deck base.*

Chapter Six

Large Detail Sets and Converting Kit Parts

The kit used for the build in this chapter is Hong Kong Models 1/32 de Havilland Mosquito Mk IX/Mk XVI. This kit is the second de Havilland Mosquito that Hong Kong Models has released, the first being the Mk IV/PR.Mk I/Mk IV series. Their innovative one-piece front and rear fuselage sections, one-piece wing and hollow flight controls make for an easy build for modellers. There is a slightly raised seam to rub down on these surfaces, but the design of the manufacture avoids having to join halves together or to glue seams to rectify.

One of the latest concepts to hit the plastic model world is the use of slide moulds. This fuselage and cockpit were moulded as one piece. There is a slightly raised ridge where the halves were joined in the mould, which a quick swipe with a sponge sander will cure.

A slide-moulded one-piece wing. All that is needed is fitting of the trailing-edge inserts and the flight controls. The wing tips and flight controls are moulded in a similar fashion.

HONG KONG MODELS 1/32 de HAVILLAND MOSQUITO MK IX/MK XVI

This build illustrates detailing using large resin detail sets, etched brass, scratch building and converting. This is an expensive kit, retailing at around £175, and the detail sets are an additional cost, so some previous experience is necessary to get the best from the outlay.

Detail sets used:

- Eduard Brassin 632-092 Mosquito MkVI port engine, resin and etched brass set. This engine is a Merlin 21 with a single stage supercharger and will be converted to a Rolls Royce Merlin 76/77. For the conversion some cross kitting was carried out with a two-speed two-stage supercharger and intercooler taken from a 1/32 Tamiya Mustang kit
- Eduard 32918 Mosquito Mk IX interior set. Etched brass

- Eduard 32417 Mosquito Mk IX exterior/engine set. Etched brass
- Eduard JX208 Mosquito Mk IX mask set. Paper tape

References used:

- *Warpaint Special No3 de Havilland Mosquito* printed by Regal Litho Ltd
- *Haynes Manual de Havilland Mosquito* ISBN 978 0 85733 360 5
- Haynes Manual Rolls-Royce Merlin engine ISBN 978 0 85733 758 0
- de *Havilland Mosquito*, an illustrated history Volume 2 by Ian Thirsk ISBN 978 0 85979 102 1

- Google images

This is a challenging project. To get the best results, a fair amount of researching and dry fitting needs to be done before any assembly is started. The kit's engines are adequate for most modellers, but they are a little soft in detail and lacking quite a few parts.

To begin the build, the kit's starboard engine was assembled with the nacelles, firewall and undercarriage. This engine was to be fully covered so there was no point adding extras in the engine-bay area. Assembling these parts first enabled a check to be made for the possibility of using the Eduard engine before committing to modifying the kit parts.

The following areas needed to be assessed, as there was a large amount of cross-kitting and modification required:

- The built-up resin engine needed to be the same overall length as the plastic one. The Eduard

engine is based on the single-stage two-speed Merlin 21. This needs to be converted to the two-stage two-speed with intercooler Merlin 76/77

- The resin bearers are for the shorter engine, so the plastic engine bearers from the kit needed to be used. Only a small adjustment was required where they fitted to the firewall
- The resin firewall needed to fit the cowlings and give the correct height to the undercarriage
- The undercarriage legs needed to be modified at the top of each leg to correspond with the new firewall
- From online pictures and books there is a small half-height firewall between the supercharger casing and the main firewall. This needed to be scratch built from plastic card and spares. There is a curved frame within the resin engine set for Merlin 21: this was used as a template for the new short firewall.

The standard kit assembly of the starboard engine and nacelle. This required assembly so comparisons could be made with the resin assembly for the port side.

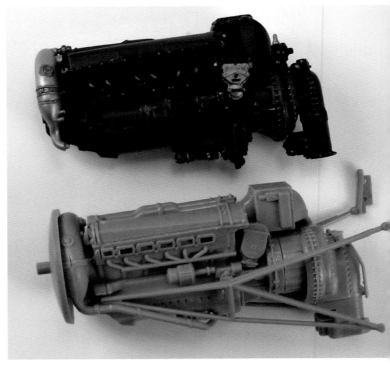

ABOVE LEFT: *The difference between a single-stage two-speed supercharger and a two-stage two-speed supercharger. The top one is from a Tamiya P-51D Mustang kit, the lower one from the Eduard resin set.*

ABOVE RIGHT: *Comparing the two engines. The upper one is the resin engine with the Tamiya supercharger fitted. Cables, pipework and engine bearers are yet to be fitted. The lower one is from the kit's engine taken straight from the box.*

The difference between the resin firewall on the left and the kit's firewall on the right. The resin firewall has two round rods that were intended for the Tamiya Mosquito kit. These were retained as the kit's undercarriage legs were hollow. By removing the lugs on the top of the kit parts, then drilling a hole with appropriate dimensions in the top of each leg, the firewall rods can be slid into each leg assembly. This will give strength to the whole leg assembly. The area outlined in red needs to be removed.

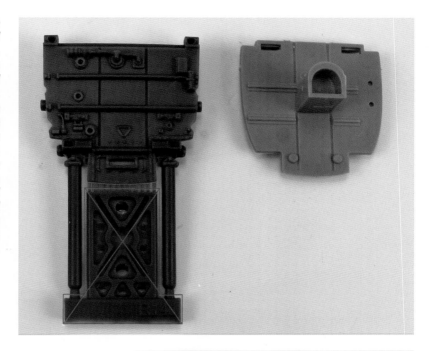

Some serious planning was needed to build the model, so the usual method of following kit instructions was avoided. Several components, such as flying controls, tail planes, flaps and undercarriage, were put together as sub-assemblies. This kind of work was done between working on the resin engine and cockpit areas. It would be possible to build the entire rear fuselage and put it to one side before concentrating on the more complex parts of the adaptations.

Work started with the Eduard resin engine. This engine is a masterpiece of casting and consists of approximately 130 parts, including pipework and wiring. The resin engine was made up for the port side, as the kit's starboard engine was assembled when checks were made for dimensions.

When all the parts for the resin engine were sorted, the casting blocks were removed. Some of the parts, especially the ducting and pipework, are fragile, so a very fine saw was used to cut the stronger parts, and a sharp knife to take care of the lighter parts that needed removing. Cutting the casting blocks off the pipework can be done while other parts are drying. Part numbers are engraved on the casting blocks, so it was important

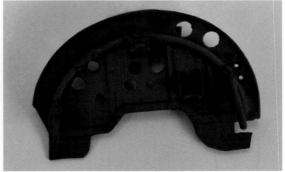

The half firewall scratch built from stock plastic sheet and strip, plus a few parts from spare etched brass sheets. Much of the firewall will be hidden by pipework, fittings and cabling.

to keep the casting block and part together for identification.

As this engine was converted there was the possibility that some of the pipework needed altering. It was therefore important to check reference material for accuracy. Online images and internet sites were used, but it is important to note that some of the pictures available show restored aircraft, which may not have the same details as the originals.

Consisting of approximately 130 parts, the Eduard engine will take patience to build but will be well worth the effort. There are some ingenious mounting methods of the parts, which makes assembly easy to get right.

Cutting off the support material needs special care. Use a very fine saw, and start by removing the main casting block. Never rush this kind of cutting, or force a saw blade: just use light pressure until you have cut through.

Once the part is removed, prepare to trim off the excess that is left on the pipe.

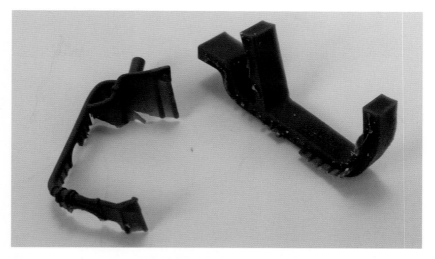

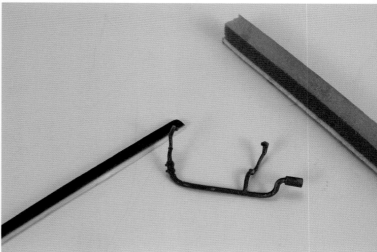

Once all the excess is removed, lightly clean up the pipe with a fine sponge sander, ready for painting.

LEFT: *The smaller pipe that comes off the main pipe is liable to break as it is a weak point. This happened with the one illustrated when cleaning it up. The break was remedied by using superglue to secure it back in place.*

ENGINE ASSEMBLY PART ONE

When all the casting blocks were removed, assembly started with gluing the spark plugs and plug-lead tube on to the cylinder banks. The banks were then glued on to the crankcase. The rear supercharger casing from the Tamiya engine was then mated up to the resin crankcase. Surprisingly, the accessories moulded on the Tamiya supercharger matched up almost perfectly to the resin crankcase. The only adjustment made to the supercharger casing was removal of the locating peg required for the Tamiya kit.

As the engine assembly progressed it would have been easy to damage parts already fitted, so a temporary engine stand was made using a block of wood and an aluminium tube to hold the engine while placing other parts. A plastic tube would have been equally effective. Placing cables of 3mm and 4mm length to the spark plugs required patience, but it was worth the effort.

There were many pipes, cables and linkages to be assembled on the engine once the engine bearers were fitted. The Eduard instructions were useful for this task, but it was necessary to bear in mind that some parts needed extending and

When the engine reached this stage, work was started on the nacelles and firewall assembly.

The basic engine assembly is complete. To make life easier, a stand was made from a block of wood and a metal tube. This was used to stop any accidental damage to some of the finer details.

some rerouting. There is a later stage of the build where the engine needs to be fitted to the firewall so the cables and pipes can be routed to their correct position in the engine bay area. This will be discussed later, after the wings and fuselage have been fitted together.

NACELLES AND FIREWALL ASSEMBLY

The next stage was to assemble the port and starboard nacelles and the firewalls. Kit and resin parts for each nacelle were assembled in parallel to provide uniform configuration between the resin firewall and the plastic nacelles. This was to ensure that the finished pieces were the same level when assembled on the airframe. The starboard nacelle was built first using just the kit parts, followed by the port nacelle using some etched parts from the Eduard exterior set. The resin firewall needed some adjustment to the sides to remove unwanted protrusions. The general shape of the

sides was a good fit to the nacelles. The undercarriage and oil-tank assemblies had to be assembled along with the nacelles.

The only problem to arise on the undercarriage was with the kit's mudguards. When assembled and compared with references, these looked as if they were too close to the wheel. These were replaced with the etched ones from the Eduard set.

When working on a major conversion, keep dry fitting and checking the model against the kit's version. In this picture you can see the modifications made to the tops of the leg, ringed in red. A few minor adjustments will ensure that everything will be at the same height.

The two nacelle units partially assembled with some of the etched parts. Everything is matching up so far. The mudguards and oil tanks are about to be fitted.

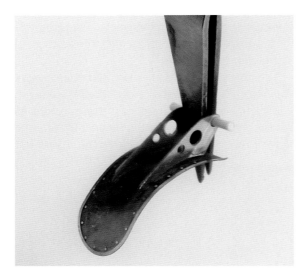

After the final assembly of the nacelles and undercarriage units, according to references the mudguards looked to be far too close to the wheels. The Eduard etched brass ones were assembled and dry fitted, but these also looked out of place, so a 5mm extension was added to make a more satisfactory appearance.

While the nacelles were drying, the wing assembly was put together. Most of the parts for this assembly are moulded in one piece. The wing trailing edges and leading edges of the flying controls needed to be added, along with aileron hinge points, centre section fuel tanks and wing tips. The nacelles could then be glued to the wing, making sure they sat in the correct position. The wing tips are also produced in one piece, so these required careful lining up on the upper and lower surface. It might be possible to add some plastic beam into the wing to avoid steps on the joining surfaces. The clear landing-light lenses and navigation light covers were left off until after painting.

THE COCKPIT

Adding additional detail to the cockpit area is not an easy task when you are dealing with a one-piece moulding. The cockpit in this kit is designed

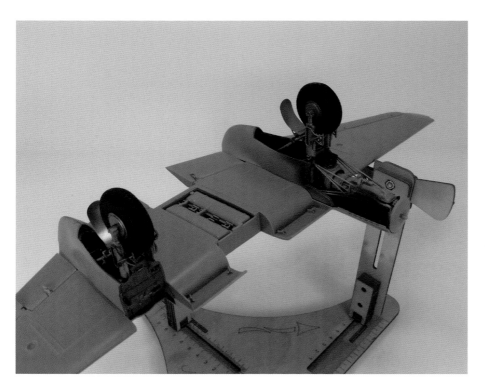

The wing assembly with the nacelles are dry fitted into place. The nacelles are a tight fit and clip into place with shaped wedges on the nacelle sides. The rear part of the nacelle must also clip over the inner and outer flap-assembly connecting rod.

to be built up as a sub-assembly and then slid into the nose area from the rear. The problem with this method is that the sub-assembly leaves a step on the front edge. Some modellers get around this by cutting the front end in half longitudinally with a fine saw. This enables the sub-assembly side walls to be glued to the cut halves, correcting the step and allowing for additional detailing.

The focus on this build was the port engine, so it was decided to use just the Eduard cockpit detail set alongside the standard kit parts. Work started by removing raised moulded-on detail such as the throttle box from the side walls and moulded detail on the instrument panel. The side wall was curved so was not easy to cut off with a knife. An electric mini drill and sanding drum was used at a slow speed to take off the greatest quantity, and then the area was finished by scraping with a small curved knife blade. The rudder pedals were moulded on to the instrument panel. These were removed and replaced with the etched brass ones from the Eduard set.

Once all the parts had the detail removed, they were primed and painted in the appropriate colours. All the colour photo etch was applied after the paint had dried. The photo etch was bonded by holding the part in position, picking up a small amount of a medium superglue on a piece of fine wire, and letting capillary action make the bond. Some panels had small spots of glue put on the plastic part and the panel placed on top. A slow-drying superglue was used, allowing the part to be manoeuvred into position.

Finally, the seat belts were attached to the seats, and the sub-assemblies making up the tub were prepared, ready to be slid into the nose section. Once the cockpit insert was dry then there were three main assemblies: the nose, the wings with nacelles, and the tail section. The nose was glued to the tail section, and when dry the wings were dry fitted to the fuselage, the symmetry was checked, and when it was considered satisfactory, the wings were glued to the fuselage. A further check was made before the glue dried in case any further adjustment was needed.

The one-piece moulded nose is impressive, but not if you wish to add more detail or make corrections in this area. For example, the assembled cockpit, when slid into place from the back, leaves a step at the front edge, which can be seen from the bomb aimer's glazing on the nose.

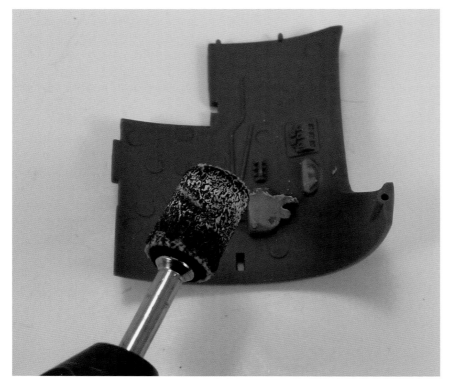

The major part of the moulded-on detail was removed using a small sanding drum in an electric mini drill at slow speed. It was then finished off by hand with a curved knife blade.

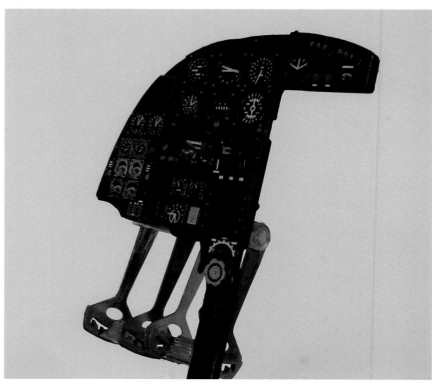

The instrument panel with replacement colour photo etch and rudder pedals.

All the cockpit assemblies are ready to be put together. Note the dirty wood area in front of the rudder pedals, and the pedals that still need painting.

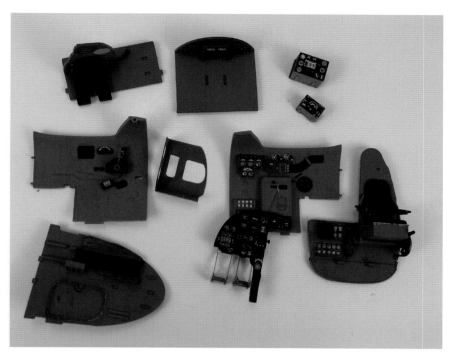

The completed nose area. Once the port side wall is attached, the assembly is glued into the nose.

The airframe is now coming together. The three main components are now glued together, and the symmetry has been checked. The port engine bay area requires work next.

ENGINE ASSEMBLY PART TWO

Once the overall symmetry was judged satisfactory, the starboard engine assembly was finished by fitting the upper, lower and side cowlings. When these were dry a measurement was taken from the back edge of the top cowling to the edge of the spinner, to be compared with the port engine once it was installed. They should both be the same at 72mm, plus or minus 1mm. The port engine main cooling pipes on the underside of the engine needed fitting before the engine was attached to the firewall, along with any other cables or fittings.

The most difficult part was fitting the engine to the firewall. Dry fitting at this stage allowed the model to be viewed from all directions, giving an opportunity for any necessary adjustments to be made to the engine bearers. Finally, the engine was glued in place using a slow-drying superglue. It is possible to tack the engine, for example, on

the top two points, giving time to set the bottom two at a slower pace or to make any more adjustments.

Only when the bulk of the pipework was satisfactorily in place was the scratch-built sub-firewall fitted. Once the sub-firewall was in place, there was a mass of wiring, tubing and connecting rods that could have been fitted, but it came to a point where it was not physically possible to add in any more detail. If, when you are faced with a similar dilemma, you feel you need to get some wires in place from an exposed point, but cannot get to where they should end, let them go in the general direction of where they should be, but finish in an area that cannot be seen.

This engine was to be fully uncovered, so the last parts fitted were the exhausts, cowling framework and finally the propeller. The cowling framework was from the Eduard exterior/engine set, and had to be adjusted as these parts were intended to fit only on to the cowlings. Only after fitting the framework for the cowlings was a manufacturer's error noticed, which demonstrates how easy it is to miss a mistake. The side cowling frames had thirty-four pairs of holes etched into them, which was intended to represent the places where cowling fasteners should go. On the real aircraft there were only nine. To make a correction, the frames were removed, and thin masking tape placed over them. The original holes could be seen through the tape, allowing new holes to be pierced and drilled with better spacing.

Another correction was necessary, as with the cowlings off, the back plate can be seen on this aircraft. Hong Kong Models did not supply spinner back plates for the propeller assembly with this kit. One was found in the box of spare parts most modellers keep, which just happened to fit the port engine.

The port engine rear firewall has had details fitted from the spares box. The wing section has had plastic card and strip added. Some holes have been drilled to accept the pipes leading to the inboard radiators.

The port engine is now fitted to the main firewall. The secondary scratch-built firewall is temporary and has been put in place to check the fit before adding some brackets and accessories. This bulkhead was not installed until further pipework and cables were fitted.

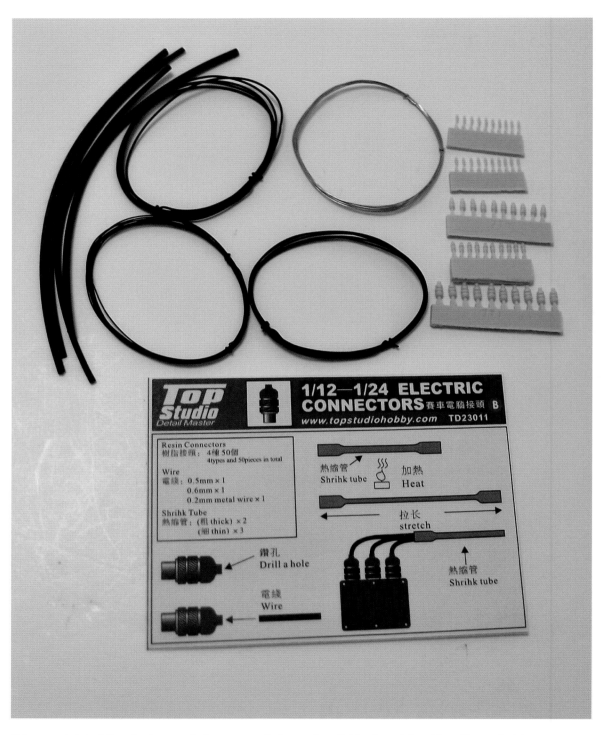

When scratch building, look around at components from other fields of model making. These electric or pipe connections for model cars were very useful. They come with wire, different-sized connectors, and heat-shrink tubing.

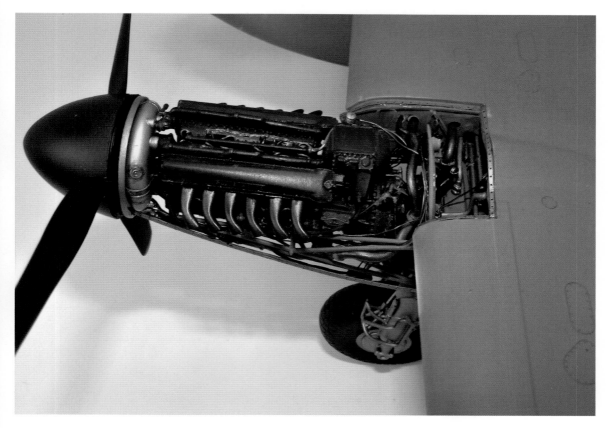

Here the engine bay is coming together, and the framework for the cowling panels is being installed.

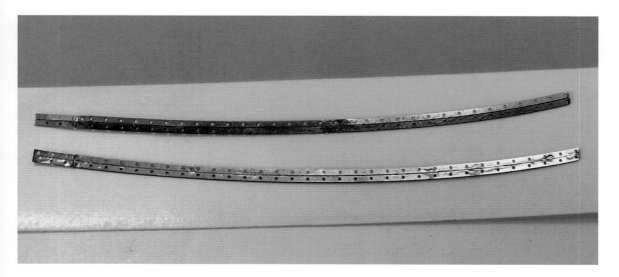

The extended brass strips from the Eduard exterior/engine set are being glued together with medium superglue. This is being done on a strip backing paper from paint mask material, which will help to stop glue leaching through gaps and bonding the brass to the assembly mat.

The cowling frames are glued in place. At this stage something did not look right, and after careful study of kit parts and references it became clear that there were too many holes.

Paper masking tape was placed over the etched holes and new holes punched through using the etched holes as a guide, but the new holes were given different spacing.

PHOTO-RECONNAISSANCE VERSION

During the build, various colour schemes were considered but nothing really caught the attention until an American photo-reconnaissance aircraft was found. To convert this aircraft to an American PR version was easy – the only extra part needed was an oblique camera port on the port side of the fuselage, as the other two ports in the bomb-bay doors are supplied in the kit. This oblique port was achieved with a piece of 6mm plastic tube. There were no plans showing the actual position, so photographs and side profiles were used to

make a fair estimation of the position. A 6mm hole was drilled in the fuselage, then a section of 6mm tube was cut and inserted into the hole, leaving it slightly proud so it could be contoured to the fuselage shape. A piece of clear acetate was then cut and placed inside the tube.

Now the decision to represent the American PR plane had been made, some sections of paint-work were started to move the project along. After priming, a white basecoat was applied to areas such as the tail and the underwing invasion stripes. All the national markings and serial numbers were painted on using custom-made paint-mask sets from Scalewarship Ltd.

A 6mm-diameter tube was inserted into the fuselage. It was left proud of the sides so it could be sanded to the fuselage profile.

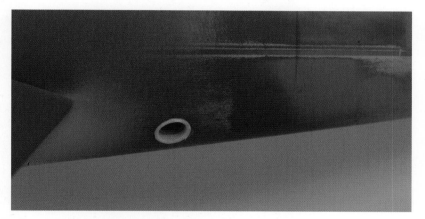

Once the decision had been taken to represent the American photo-reconnaissance version, some areas were painted between assembly stages. The whole tail section was completed as one task.

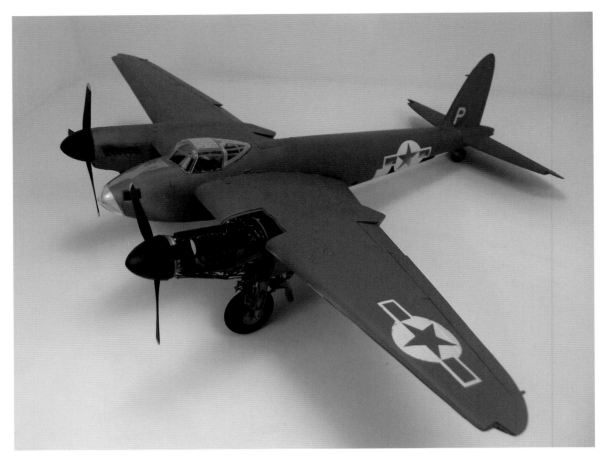

ABOVE: *Isolated areas were painted white for the invasion stripes, then the paint masks for the star and bars were applied ready for the insignia blue.*

The new oblique camera port, lower fuselage invasion stripes and insignia were completed. The invasion stripes are arguably too neat – some wartime photographs show them to be uneven and poorly applied.

FINAL TOUCHES
AND CONCLUSION

The overall paint scheme finish is RAF PRU blue. This was applied using Vallejo air acrylic paint, and done in sections. This is not an ideal way to apply paint, but it is convenient when applying it to parts of the final build. The canopy, nose blister and side windows were glued in place prior to painting those areas. All the other transparencies for lights were completed after all the painting was finished.

While painting the canopy, an unusual event occurred. The transparent canopy panels were all separate and were glued on to the interior frame. It was intended to paint on black first, then move on to paint the PRU blue. The black went into a small gap where panels joined, and capillary action took place, moving the black into where the exterior panel touched the interior frame. Unfortunately, nothing could be done about this because of the location. The separate panels were securely glued down so there was no access. While annoying, the error would be easily overlooked, but it is worth mentioning so that other builders can avoid the same mistake.

Other final parts fitted included the wing leading-edge radiators, and the etched brass front and rear faces as supplied on the Eduard exterior set. The plastic radiators in the kit were painted matt black, and the etched front and rear faces were painted a burnt-iron colour. This gives some contrast with the matt black, which visually adds depth once they are glued in place. The pilot's access hatch under the nose had been painted separately, then assembled and was put in place. The main undercarriage doors were assembled, painted and glued in place, along with the aerial mast that completed the

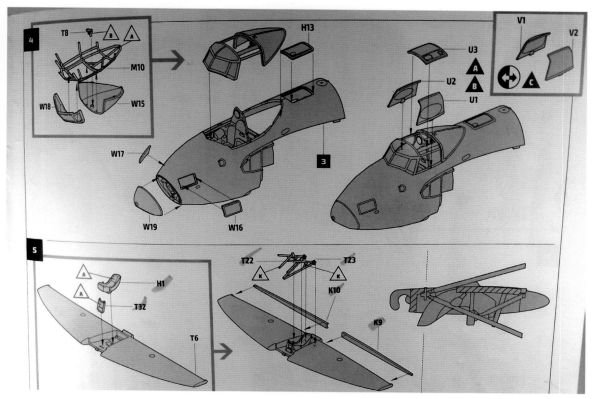

The instruction sheet showing the assembly of the canopy. The inner frame must be painted first before attaching the outer transparencies.

The annoying issue of capillary action. Between the canopy frame and the transparency, the black undercoat seeped into a small gap where the transparent panels join.

The completed project viewed from aft.

assembly of this aircraft. A small amount of weathering was applied to hinge points and access panels and some exhaust staining on the lower nacelles.

This project was an enjoyable one, but not without difficulties. The engine conversion was a gamble and at times frustrating, but the result was worth the extra effort. There are many more options for detailing this kit, especially if the bomb-bay doors were opened. The kit contains the pieces necessary for this option.

The completed project with the engine detail visible.

Chapter Seven

Assembling a Complete Multimedia Kit

The kit used for the project in this chapter is the Aviatik Berg D.1 Engine Section, an HpH Models multimedia kit. Extra details came from a custom-made etch fret, described in Chapter 2.

This is a true multimedia kit made up from wood, etched brass, polyurethane resin and decals. HpH Models produce some highly detailed kits using many different mediums. This complex type of kit should not be attempted until you have

some experience of using multimedia compo-nents. The instructions are step-by-step pictures, with nothing written. The pictures show how to proceed, although some sections would have benefited from the inclusion of some dimen-sions, or basic written instruction. The instruction book starts with numbered pictures of the parts. Unfortunately the etch fret is numbered incor-rectly in some places, but this is not too much of

The HPH Aviatik Berg D1 kit parts spread out, including the replacement cylinders made in Chapter 2. This is a truly multimedia kit with wood, resin and etched brass. It makes into a nice rendition of the engine bay and part of the cockpit.

The instruction booklet pictures are clear enough, but a bit more information regarding some parts would be of benefit. For example, there are no dimensions given on the profiles and brackets on which the oil tank sits (the area ringed with red circles). It is then necessary to gauge from the picture and dry fit these parts with the tank.

a problem as the parts are easily identified during placement.

THE AUSTRO-DAIMLER ENGINE

The first thing to take care of is cleanliness. As with all resin kits, it is necessary to wash all the resin parts in warm soapy water. This helps to remove any silicon release agent that may be present on the resin parts. Assembly starts with the engine sump and crankcase, which are solid resin parts. The two gluing faces were keyed up with a medium-grade sanding stick, or wet-and-dry paper on a flat surface: this was necessary because resin can be so smooth that it forms a barrier to bonding. After sanding, five-minute

epoxy glue was used to bond these parts, which allowed time to manoeuvre the two parts together.

It was important to ensure that all the bolt heads and tails lined up correctly. The original cylinders supplied in the kit had some serious mould defects, so a silicon mould was made, and six new cylinders were cast in resin. The process of casting from original parts is detailed in Chapter 2. The cylinders and the assembled crankcase were primed and painted separately, giving more control over the painting and detailing.

As many of the small parts are mounted on a flat resin plate, they required careful removal with a fine-cut razor saw. There are several companies producing etched saw blades – the ones used are by RB Productions and come in various shapes suitable for getting into places

When gluing resin parts together, use a slow-drying glue such as five-minute epoxy. Abrade the two surfaces with a medium-grade sanding stick, making sure both surfaces are flat. The slow-drying nature of the adhesive gives you a chance to line up everything correctly before it sets.

The crankcase and cylinders after painting. The instructions recommended that the cooling jacket (the top part of the cylinders) should be copper. However, an online search on the Austro-Daimler engine suggested that the copper cooling jacket was replaced with a welded steel jacket, so a burnt-steel colour was used instead of copper.

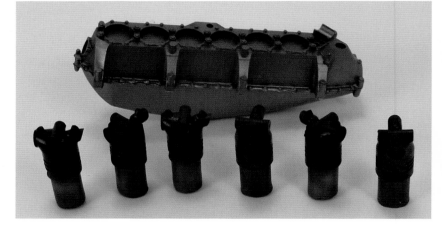

that would otherwise be very difficult to access. Most of these blades will fit into standard craft-knife handles.

Some of the parts on the plate, even with careful treatment, were under-sized when cut and so required replacement. Glass beads were used as an alternative for the under-sized parts. The resin cylinders needed to have a 0.5mm hole drilled through the top to take a brass rod, so the glass beads were used to act as spacers between the cylinders. When drilling the cylinders, it was necessary to drill from both sides so as not to drill at an angle. There is a punch mark to show where to drill from.

The overhead cam case and accessories were assembled and fitted. After assembling all the rocker arms on to the cam case, a close examination revealed that something did not look quite right. The manufacturer, HpH, has cast all the rocker arms at the same angles, but really, they should be at different angles depending on the stroke of the piston. This may be a pedantic point, but in this scale it is noticeable. Because the fault was not identified until after gluing was complete, it was too late to get the correct look for this model. Correction would involve changing all the arms and making springs at different heights.

Different-shaped saw blades made in etch are very useful when removing small items that have been cast on to plates. Problems can arise with such small items – for example, by the time the small round discs seen here were cut off, the saw cut made them too small for the gap in which they were designed to fit. Other fittings shown include spark plugs, valve rockers with springs and clamps to go on to the rocker cover.

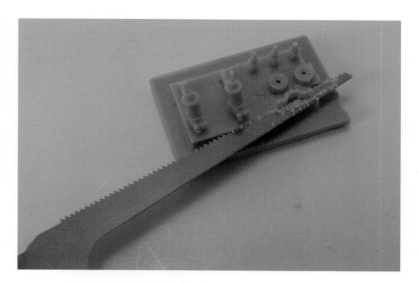

The assembled cylinders and crankcase with the brass rod and beads in place. Now is the time to do the weathering on the crankcase and cylinders, before putting on any further details that may get in the way.

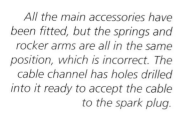

All the main accessories have been fitted, but the springs and rocker arms are all in the same position, which is incorrect. The cable channel has holes drilled into it ready to accept the cable to the spark plug.

In this view you can see cables coming out of the drilled holes to the spark plug, and the illusion of the cables from the magneto going into the channel. In fact this is solid.

One further deviation from the instructions was to fit cables from the magnetos to the spark plugs via the cable channel. This involved drilling holes into the cable channel and magnetos. The rest of the accessories were painted and fitted to complete the engine. It would be possible, with more referencing and some scratch building, to further enhance the engine bay and engine.

FUSELAGE WOODWORK

Before cutting any wood from the two laser-cut sheets it was necessary to decide what colour was wanted for the wood. In the illustrated model, Tamiya clear orange was used, which gave a varnished look to the wood. Commercial wood stains can also be used.

The laser-cut parts are held in place on the fret with a few stubs, which needed cutting to release the part from the sheet. Where the laser cuts through the wood it leaves a burn mark around the edge of the part. These burn marks can be sanded away, but the decision was taken with this model to leave them alone as they gave some definition.

HpH give a supply of wood strips to be used to build up a framework on the side pieces to fit to the frames, and to attach to the frames themselves. No measurements are given for this, so a careful study of the pictures in the instructions is necessary. When the frames were fitted, they needed to be set square to the side frames and attached, on this model using superglue. Superglue on wood bonds extremely well. Other glues such as PVA or epoxy glue can be used. These are slower drying, so the frames will need clamping or supporting while the glue dries.

When all the frames and side pieces were assembled and dry, the ammunition box was assembled and glued in place. The instrument panel was dry fitted and checked to see if it could be taken in and out again to enable the fitting of instruments and other items. At this stage the oil and fuel tanks were painted, and the brass clamps fitted. These were all glued in place with five-minute epoxy glue.

The lower surface etched brass access panel and cockpit floor were fitted next, along with the rudder bar. The engine bearers can either be glued to the frames or to the engine. On this model they were glued to the frames.

The kit includes only two instruments and two decals for the faces, with other instruments left out of the kit. The two instrument gauges were primed and painted, but the instrument decals

The bare wood was treated with a coat of Tamiya clear orange to give that varnished wood look seen on many early aircraft.

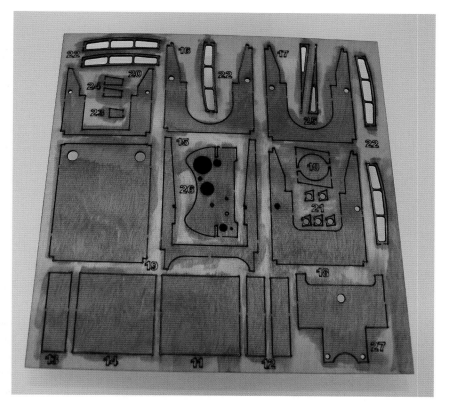

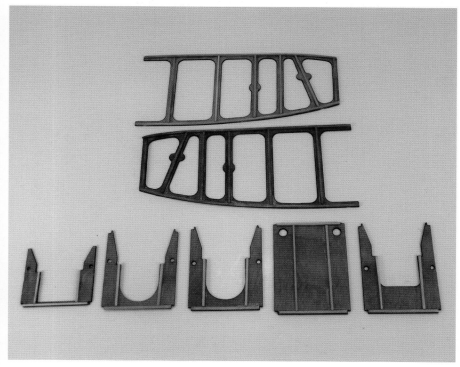

Application of the wood strips to which to fit the frames.

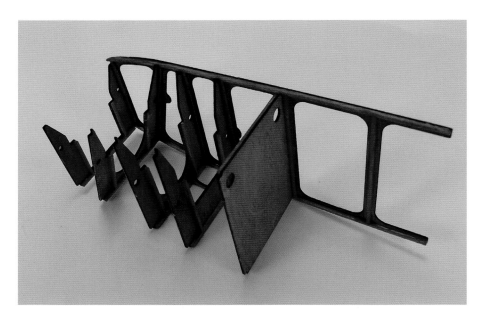

When attaching the frames make sure they are square to the side pieces. The aid of a set square can be employed, or a block if there is a shortage of space between frames.

fragmented into many pieces, because no carrier film had been incorporated over the printed decal. To get around the problem an airscale 1/32-scale sheet of World War I instruments was resized on a standard home printer. The adjusted images were carefully cut out and glued on to the resin instrument. A clear acetate disc was placed over the image to simulate the glass face.

The last parts fitted on the cockpit section were the gun mounting frames and plates.

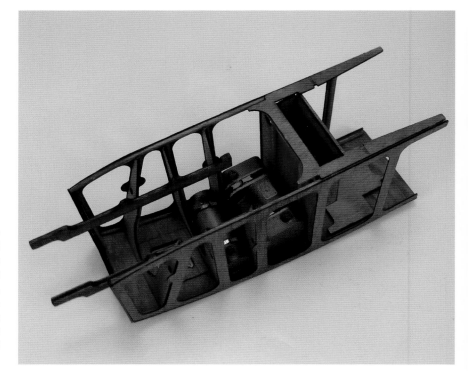

The basic engine bay area with fuel and oil tanks installed. Notice how the burn marks highlight areas. A small amount of oil-coloured wash was introduced to a few areas, so the wood did not look so new.

This is what happens when there is no carrier film over the printed decal: the decal just falls apart.

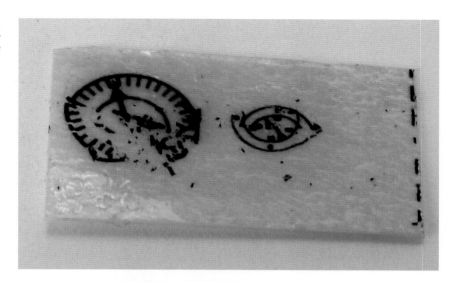

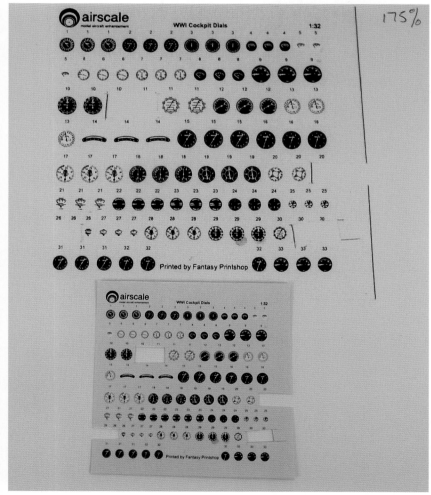

To overcome the problem of the fragmented decal, a 1/32-scale decal sheet was enlarged on a home printer by 175 per cent. The finished print came very close to the size required.

The instrument panel, once completed, is glued into place, followed by the framework, which holds the two guns. The guns will be fitted at a later stage.

THE WING SECTION AND FINAL ASSEMBLY

The final stages of construction dealt with the centre section of the wing, which was built up from laser-cut ribs, front and rear spars, leading edge and trailing edge parts. Again, the instructions give no measurement guides as to where the ribs go, but this was not too much of a problem as a study of the parts and the pictures gave adequate indication. There are two skins for the wing section top and bottom. These skins provide the correct width of the wing section, and indicate where the ribs are to be placed.

Associated with the wing section are the struts: these come on a resin plate and have a piece of wire going through them to stop them from bending. The instructions indicate the struts should be inserted directly into the wood. On real aircraft they would be attached to metal plates, but none are supplied with the kit.

The instructions also suggest the struts be put on the wrong way round, but the instructions also have two pictures of real aircraft showing the correct location.

The photo etch set produced in Chapter 2 includes the plates and strut connections missing from the kit, but needed for greater accuracy on this model. The two front and two rear struts were replaced with white metal ones with a better shape and size, sourced from the spares box. All the plates and brackets were painted black, and the struts a grey/green shade. These were then assembled on to the airframe. The lower fittings on the struts were held in place with a 0.5mm brass rivet, and tacked in place with superglue.

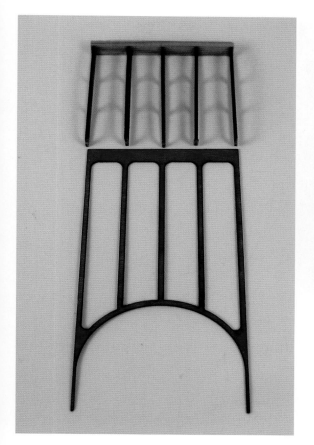

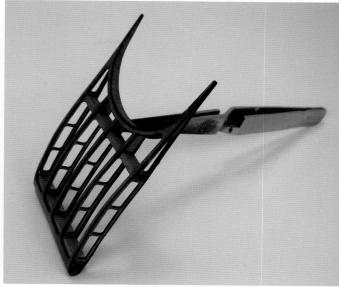

ABOVE: *After sanding the leading edge into shape, the wing assembly is now complete, except for the etched brackets that accept the struts.*

LEFT: *There are two skins for the wing section, an upper and a lower one. These are used to mark out and place the ribs, so that when the skins are in place the ribs line up with them.*

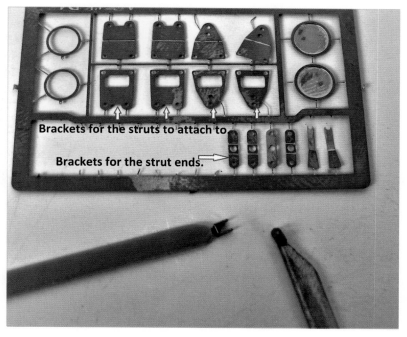

Brackets for the struts to attach to

Brackets for the strut ends.

The etch set made in Chapter 2 was used to make the end fittings for the struts. The brackets, into which the struts fit, were absent from the kit.

In the final stages of assembly the guns were placed on to the gun supports, and the struts assembled on to the wing section. The struts are quite difficult to line up and put on to the wing. The solution chosen to ease the process was to tack the lower parts of the struts in place and then attach the wing section.

Getting all six struts equal and lined up was a bit of a challenge but eventually, after some juggling with the wing section, the main part of the build was complete.

THE PROPELLER

The final parts to fit were the propeller and centre boss. These were supplied as a cast resin piece. Scrutiny of the centre section of the propeller revealed a faint centre point, which needed to be drilled out to accept the propeller shaft. Once done, the propeller was primed and painted. Artists' profile pictures of the Aviatik usually show the propeller with distinctly different wood lamination colours, whereas photographs of the real thing commonly show the colour of the wood laminations to be one shade. A dark wood colour was chosen, and some graining applied using a stencil in a slightly darker shade.

The front and rear centre boss plates were painted an aluminium colour and glued in place with five-minute epoxy. The epoxy allowed time to manoeuvre the front and back pieces so they lined up correctly. There was no stand supplied with the

kit, so a spare airliner stand was assembled and attached to the bottom skin.

This is a true multimedia kit, which on balance assembled very well. Further improvements to the basic kit could be added with additional research and detailing.

The propeller base colour is painted in Lifecolor raw sienna. This was then darkened with a touch of black, and airbrushed through a stencil for the wood grain effect. One coat of satin clear coat added depth to the overall appearance.

The propeller hub is painted aluminium, and an oil wash is applied around all the nuts to bring out the detail.

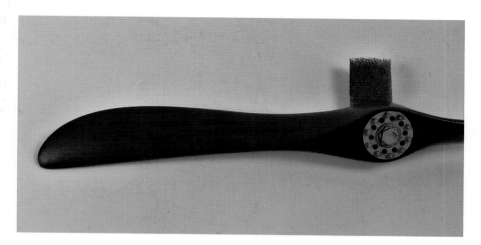

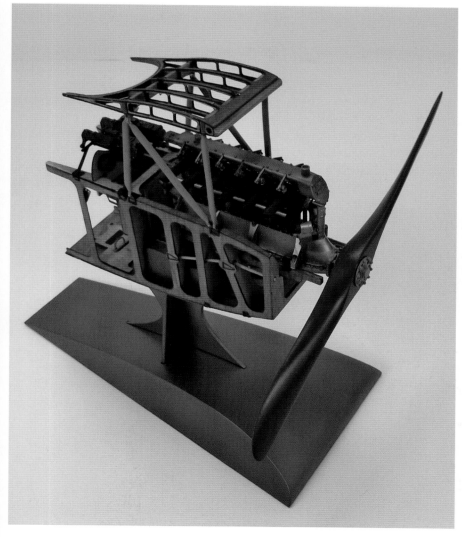

The result is an attractive display piece.

Chapter Eight

Replacing Major Parts of the Plastic Kit with Resin and Etched Brass

The kit used for the build in this chapter is Revell Fw 190 F8 kit number 04869. The aircraft depicted was built in the later part of World War II when paint stocks were low. The fuselage and lower surfaces were bare metal with some light mottling, simplified national markings, and virtually non-existent stencilling. The fabric tail surfaces were covered in red dope.

The real aircraft has a heart-warming story to it. EagleCals instruction sheet informs us that on 8 May 1945 pilot Eugen Lorcher belly-landed this aircraft near his home town Aufhausen to escape the

DETAIL SETS USED

- Eduard Big Sin Fw 190 F8 Part 1: cockpit, machine gun mounting bay, and flaps Big Sin 63206
- Eduard Brassin engine set ED632063
- Eduard Brassin bronze undercarriage legs and resin doors ED632 057
- Eduard resin wheels ED632 055
- Eduard propeller set ED632 069
- Master-model brass pitot tube and MG151 barrels AM-32-065
- Master-model brass MG-131 barrels and cooling jackets AM-32-003
- EagleCals EC166 alternative decals

advancing Russian forces. On board was his fiancée, who was riding in the radio compartment located in the rear fuselage. The couple had a low-level flight, taking fire but managing to land without injury; both walked away. 'Every year on this anniversary he and his wife returned to this site and celebrated their escape with a toast of champagne.'

This build is another challenging one, but made easier as most of the detail sets are from Eduard's Big Sin or Brassin ranges. These sets were designed for use with the Revell kit so they should fit well, making the build straightforward. An important point to make here is that a large part of the plastic kit will be replaced with resin. Some of the pieces, like the engine and the cockpit, are made from a considerable quantity of resin, which is heavier than plastic. This puts a lot of strain on flimsy plastic undercarriage legs, which is why the bronze undercarriage legs from Eduard have been used.

The reason for using all this additional detail is to demonstrate the build of the aircraft itself. Most of the panels and cowlings, from the cockpit forward, open on hinges, so that it is possible to see much more of the detail behind them. As mentioned before, modern detail sets are very accurate and well detailed, allowing a much truer representation.

BMW 801 ENGINE

Because of the complexity of the engine, it was decided to make it the first part of the build. There

Separate from the basic Revell kit, these eight detail sets were used to add a plethora of accurate details. The bronze undercarriage was really needed to support the weight of all the resin and etched brass.

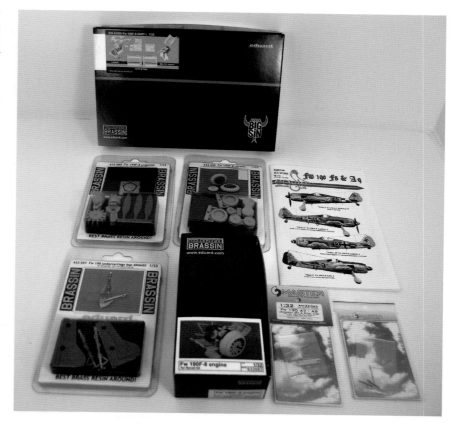

were natural breaks during which it was possible to start on the cockpit and other parts to advance the rest of the build. In common with the Eduard Merlin engine, this BMW engine has in excess of 130 parts to it, all needing to be cut away from casting blocks. Be aware that some parts needed to be cut leaving some resin in place to act as a locater on to other parts. It is possible to miss this requirement on the instructions.

With some of the resin parts, the cut faces needed to be flat and square, otherwise there would be problems later when assembling the whole unit. Time was taken to rotate the parts when cutting and sanding, which helped get a straight cut and a flat surface. During sanding, only a small amount was attempted at any one time, and a regular check was made on the surface to keep the part true.

It can be very difficult to ensure that radial engine cylinders are square and true. Usually the cylinders are round at the base so can be twisted

easily from the correct position. Eduard have fixed this problem by including two templates in etched brass which help to keep the cylinders true and with correct spacing between each cylinder.

This engine warrants careful painting to bring out the exquisite detail, so it is worth taking plenty of time. All the cylinders were painted individually using acrylic aluminium, dark aluminium, black and an oil wash before assembling on to the crankcases.

Gradually the engine came together as two main assemblies, the front and back halves. It would be quite easy to misalign the two parts when putting them together. There only needs to be a couple of degrees of misalignment to affect the fit of cowlings and exhaust positions later in the build, so care was taken to ensure a good fit. Once all the etched spark-plug leads were fitted, the rear main frame and exhausts could be fitted. The lower exhausts were left loose so adjustments could be made later if this proved necessary.

The engine parts removed from the box. Note that the cylinders and crankcase parts have been separated and put into separate bags. All the parts are clearly marked, but once removed from the casting blocks they can get mixed up.

Pay attention to instructions when cutting off the casting blocks. Some of the items require some resin to be left in place for locating into other parts, as seen here. Note the broken induction pipe: this was an accidental breakage during the removal of the casting block. Fortunately the break was a clean one, and the pipe was superglued back in place.

Setting up the cylinders using the template supplied in the engine set. Even though the template holds the cylinders in place and there is a large locating block, there can still be movement, so take your time with this process.

BELOW: *When the two main engine components are glued together, they are located by an etched brass circle PE10, which marries up with tabs on the rear part and shaped cut-outs corresponding with the front part.*

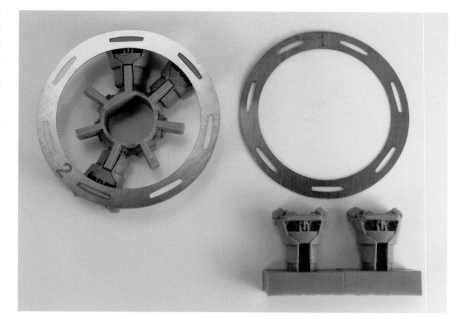

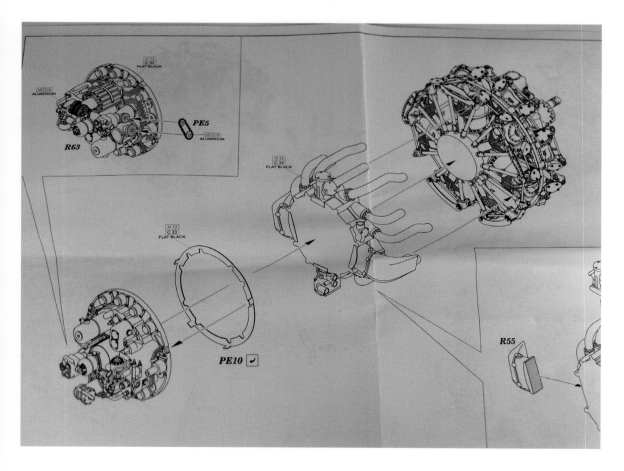

Many of the parts were painted first and then assembled. Several shades of aluminium and black were used, which gave more depth and avoided a monotone look. A small amount of oil-coloured wash was then applied to selected areas.

The rear view of the engine with the exhausts and ignition wiring fitted, together with a main frame and engine bearers. At this point, after some dry fitting to the bulkhead to check the fit of the engine, building was stopped in order to advance the fuselage.

The instructions indicate the nose cowling, cooling fan and engine bearers should be fitted next, but with this build some alterations to the fuselage panels were going to be made, so the engine build was halted after fitting the engine bearers. The fitting of the nose cowling and cooling fan is described later.

FUSELAGE AND COCKPIT

The kit's instructions inform that the two fuselage halves can be joined together after assembling and installing the tail-wheel assembly. The entire cockpit assembly is to be installed from the underside. During drying times of other components, the tail surfaces were assembled, primed and put to one side.

The Eduard cockpit is made up of a mixture of resin and etched brass. Usually Eduard include coloured photo-etched panels, but with this kit they have used resin panels and separate decals for instruments. These worked out well. They fitted easily, and the manufacturer gave extra parts in case anything was spoiled in the build. The other cockpit components, rudder pedals, seat and control stick were all assembled without problems, and with application of painted detail and weathering, the cockpit came together very quickly. Eduard supplied a fret of pre-coloured seatbelts.

Some parts of this fret looked to be slightly over scale, especially the lap straps. This may be because they are made of brass and so are not as flexible as some of the simulated fabric ones. Their application made the seat look slightly overcrowded.

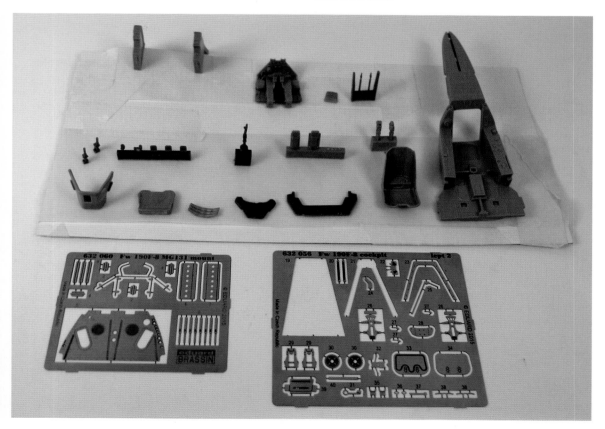

Most of the contents for the cockpit and gun platform have been set out for priming and painting.

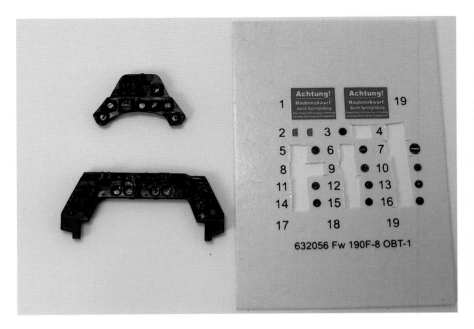

The completed instrument panels. The panels were painted RLM66 black/grey, and some of the bezels were painted satin black, which gave some contrast to an otherwise plain instrument panel.

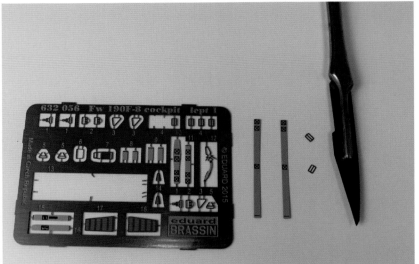

The pre-coloured seat-belt set from Eduard. These can look effective – they are better than a decal, but not as good as some of the fabric sets available.

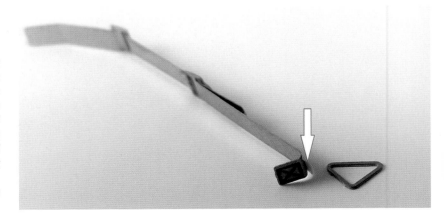

One problem you can get with pre-painted seat belts is shown here: while bending the belt to accept the shown metal part, the paint parted from the strap. Sometimes you can get it to bond down again with glue, at other times it will break off, requiring matching up with paint and touching up.

The completed cockpit, ready to be installed into the fuselage. In comparison to more modern aircraft the cockpit is quite bare. The aircraft's designer Kurt Tank designed it to be simple and easy to use.

WINGS AND PAINTING

The wings needed to have some preparatory work done to accept the etched brass flaps. Any moulded ribs from the upper wing surface and any raised edge from the lower surface needed to be scraped off and sanded smooth. The firewall is designed to be attached to a wing spar in the kit, helping to keep the wing dihedral. Some detail needed removing from the upper part so the etched brass version could be glued in place. Holes needed to be drilled out for the retractable step, for the centre-line pylon and any wing pylons that would be fitted.

Once all these were done there were some etched brass brackets and trays for the ammunition boxes to be glued on to the firewall. When those were completed the lower wing could be assembled with the firewall and spar assembly, undercarriage bays and doubler plate (plastic part 49).

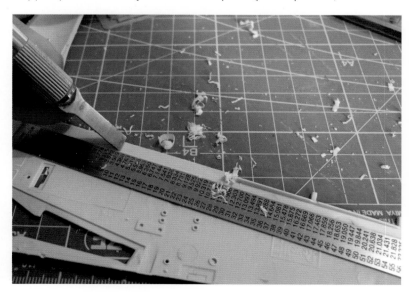

The wing lower surface being scraped to remove the raised trailing edge. The same method was used on removing the moulded-on ribs on the wing upper surfaces.

The firewall and spar glued into position. The etched brass plate is in position on the upper section, and the doubler plate can be seen behind the firewall and the spar.

This set of flaps is one of the more complex sets available. Assembly involves embossing, multiple folds, a curved leading edge on the upper plate, and separate spar. The prepared flaps are temporarily placed in position on the port wing; the moving part of the flap is not glued until final assembly.

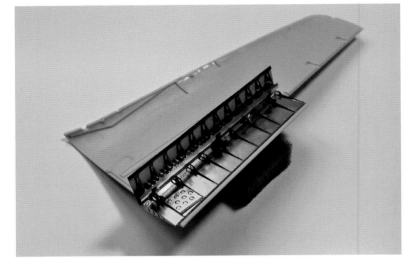

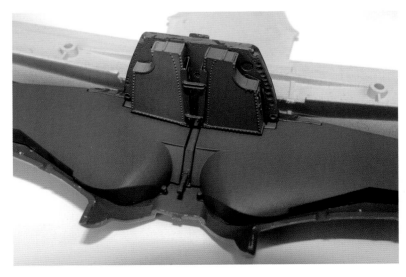

The lower wing assembly is now complete with undercarriage bays, lower engine mount and ammunition box assemblies. It has been primed and painted in RLM 02 interior grey-green.

Before fitting the wing to the fuselage, it was noted that the port and starboard vent panels on the real aircraft also hinged down, enabling a better view of the engine accessory area. A decision was made to cut these off and have them in the 'down' position. Even though the fuselage had been glued together at this point, with careful cutting this could still be achieved but it would have been easier had the adjustment been made before gluing the fuselage together.

Having ensured that the front and rear wing fillet joints lined up correctly, the lower wing assembly was dry fitted to the fuselage. The doubler plate assisted with locating components into place. The only discrepancy found with this build was with the rear parts of the wing fillets on both sides of the fuselage. The lower wing parts of the fillet protruded from both sides by approximately 1mm. As everything else lined up, the decision was taken to glue the wing in

Two vent panels have just been cut off, even though the fuselage halves had been glued together. A small razor-saw blade in a knife handle was used to achieve this.

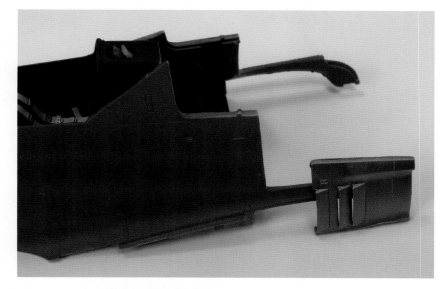

The lower wing when dry fitted to the fuselage showed a slight discrepancy, indicated by the arrow. This was only a small mismatch: at its widest point it was 1mm. Rather than trying to force out the fuselage to match up to the wings, it was decided to glue the wings into position and fill with putty.

place and use a small amount of putty on these areas.

Another option would be to put a piece of sprue runner or a piece of tube across, pushing out the sides slightly. However, the difficulty with this technique is that the cockpit bond might be weakened, or a distortion created elsewhere. Once the lower wing bond was dry, the upper wings had the upper flap section glued in place with a medium superglue. Then the wings were attached to the lower wings and fuselage. The fit was reasonably good, requiring only a few minor gaps to be filled. The tail planes that were assembled earlier were then glued in place, and when dry, the cockpit, nose section, flaps and undercarriage bays were masked off and the airframe primed.

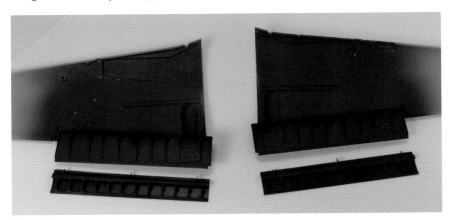

The upper wings with the built-up flaps painted and ready to be fitted to the lower wings. The lower part of the flaps will be one of the last items to be glued in place during final assembly.

After priming, check over the airframe for any faults or gaps that require filling.

The next step was to apply the camouflage scheme. As stated earlier, shortages of paint and the urgency to get aircraft out to the Luftwaffe units meant some aircraft only had paint applied to the upper surfaces. National markings and stencils were kept to a minimum, if any were applied at all. The model had various shades of aluminium applied to the fuselage and to all the lower surfaces. After painting the lower surfaces with aluminium, there were noticeable marks around the large panel on both wings. This is where Revell made alterations to the wings to represent different versions of aircraft. Because primer has a high viscosity, these marks were not initially visible through the coat of primer.

Because aluminium paint shows up the smallest flaw, the area was further treated by abrading with 1,200-grit wet-and-dry paper, and two further coats of aluminium paint were applied.

The top surfaces had the camouflage patterns applied, then a gloss clear coat was applied to make the surface ready for the national markings and stencils. After the markings were completed, a matt clear coat was applied to the complete airframe painting.

The lower surfaces and fuselage after applying various shades of aluminium.

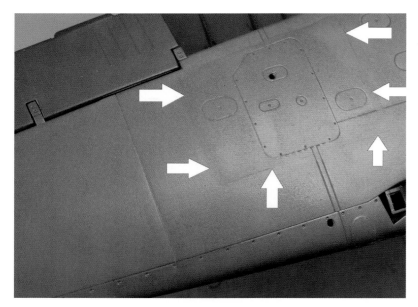

After closer inspection of the lower wings, there was a noticeable shadow line on port and starboard wings. This is where the manufacturer altered the moulds for other versions. Aluminium paint has a tendency to highlight such marks. After flatting and repainting they disappeared. Had the wings been painted the standard RLM 76 colour, it is likely the marks would not have been visible.

Gloss clear coat has been applied, on to which the decals will be placed.

The decals are all in place, and the first coat of matt varnish has been applied.

SMALL SUB-ASSEMBLIES

While the paint was drying there were a few sub-assemblies that could be built ready for installation. Those used on this model were the propeller, undercarriage and wheel sets from the Brassin range, and the machine gun and pitot tube sets from Master-Model. The bronze undercarriage set was considered a requirement for this build. With all the resin and etched brass installed on this aircraft the overall weight when built was 154g, whereas a similar size aircraft from the standard plastic kit is around 75g. The bronze legs are beautifully cast and required very little clean-up; however, the resin undercarriage doors needed to have the casting blocks removed. Care was taken with this task as parts of the doors are fragile.

The accompanying wheel set was also used because it has much more accurate detail. The assembly was simple. Both sides of the wheel had different size depths that corresponded with the thickness of the inner and outer wheel hubs. When fully built and painted, the undercarriage was installed in the wings using medium super-glue. The retraction mechanism from the plastic kit finished off the undercarriage.

The propeller assembly consists of the following parts:

• Propeller hub
• Fan disc
• Spinner
• Three blades
• One etched brass template
• Resin jig for the blades

Three Brassin sets will be used to make up the undercarriage and propeller assemblies.

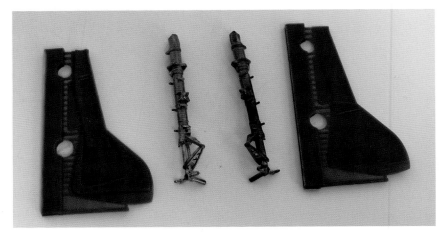

Bronze undercarriage legs are needed to support the large amount of resin and etched brass going into this kit.

The resin wheels set has been made to show bulged weight on the tyres, a manufacturer's mark, and the size of the tyres embossed on the side walls. With a bit of dry brushing these will show up well.

The basic units are made up, ready to instal into the wings.

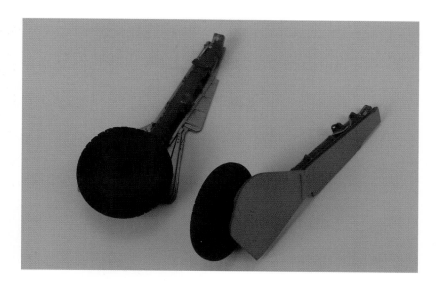

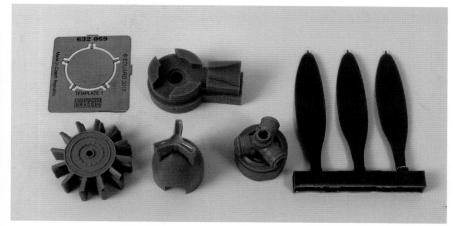

The propeller hub parts including the etch template and jig.

ABOVE LEFT: *Cutting the propeller hub from the casting block needs to be done carefully. This picture shows how the part was rotated during cutting. The hub part will need just a small amount of sanding to get it flat and smooth.*

ABOVE RIGHT: *Once the casting block is removed, the centre point will need locating for the shaft. This is where the etched brass template comes in useful. Place the disc on to the hub back plate and bend the tabs over, and then drill a pilot hole through the hole in the middle of the template.*

The propeller building jig helps to place the blades at the correct pitch. Because of the way it has been made it can't go wrong. When the blade fits snuggly into the jig, the angle is correct, and the blade is just pushed into the hub.

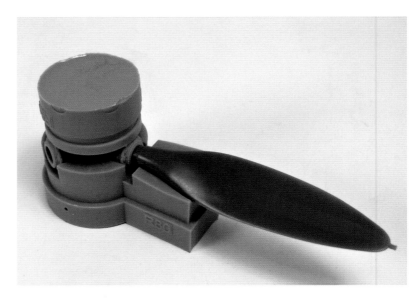

ABOVE LEFT: *The back view of the finished propeller showing the decals on the back of the blades, and the hole made with the aid of the template.*

ABOVE RIGHT: *The front view of the propeller. The spinner is in place, and the spiral decal has been applied. The fan-blade disc was cut from the casting block but put to one side until the cowling ring is fitted.*

As can be expected from a Brassin set, the detail is very good. The inclusion of templates and jig made assembly easy. There were two complex cuts to carry out: the fan-blade casting block and the hub casting block. The fan blades were very fragile, so great care was taken when cutting. The piece was rotated as it was cut to ensure an even, flat cut.

Brass barrels and pitot heads are usually straightforward replacements of kit parts. The

Master's MG131 barrels: the quality and precision are outstanding.

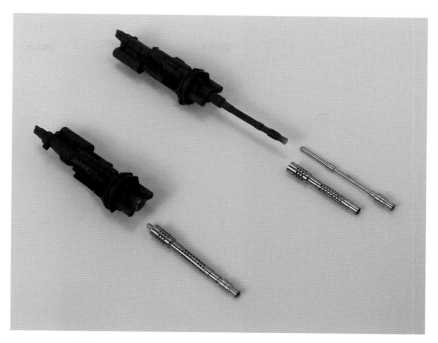

The MG151/20 wing root cannons feed through the undercarriage bay. They consist of one brass tube and one turned-down brass rod. The pitot head is turned-down brass rod and is accurate in profile. The ends of a pitot tube are usually heated to stop ice building up inside the tube: if that should happen it would affect the airspeed instrument.

quality of brass barrels readily outstrips what can be achieved with either plastic or resin casting. Some may need assembly; brass can be soldered, but usually a thin or medium superglue is used, and is just as effective.

FINAL ENGINE AND COWLINGS ASSEMBLY

After the matt clear coat was dry, the engine assembly was dry fitted to the firewall. The engine bearers all lined up well, so the assembly was glued in place with medium superglue. The machine gun mount was fitted next. Unfortunately this seemed to be slightly undersized, there being approximately a 1mm gap each side. This was filled with a piece of plastic beam. Everything else in this area fitted very well, so the logical conclusion to be drawn about the gaps is that the gun mount is undersized.

There are two cheek panels (kit parts 37 and 38), with elongated blisters on them. These locate

When the varnish was dry, test fitting the engine showed that the engine bearers lined up perfectly well. The engine assembly was finally glued in place.

At this stage the nose cowling and cheek panels have been fitted. Note also that the windscreen, gun cover and MG131 guns are in place.

on to the front part of the wing fairings and lead to the locating lugs on the resin cowling ring. Using a slow-drying superglue, the panels were glued to the fairings, and at the same time the cowling ring was matched to and attached to the engine. The assembly was then put to one side to allow the glue to dry fully.

The four main cowling panels painted earlier with other sub-assemblies were weathered at this stage to avoid any damage, as they are fragile once fitted. Once weathered, the etched brass cowling fasteners were folded up and attached to the appropriate cowling, and the cowlings attached to the aircraft. There is a gun trough panel that fits over the top of the engine. This was deliberately left off to expose more of the engine detail.

Finally, the two vent panels were weathered. The outside face of these panels on the real aircraft would get very hot from adjacent exhaust pipes, so on the model they were given a burnt look. This was also replicated on the inside face.

The last parts of the cowlings to fit were the cable stays. The parts are found on the engine etch fret. Etched cable stays are notorious for sustaining damage, and if they do get damaged, they do not look taut when in place. A successful alternative is to use the end fittings and replace the cable part with EZ line. EZ line is an elasticated thread which is attached to the end fitting and glued on to the engine, then the thread is stretched and attached to the cowling using a small dot of medium superglue.

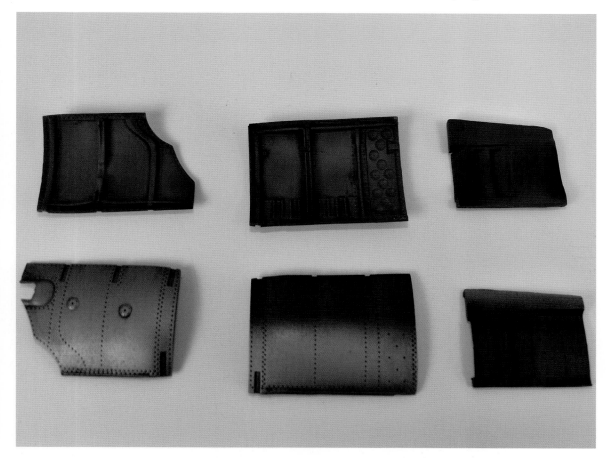

The six main panels that cover the engine were painted separately and then weathered with an oil-coloured wash.

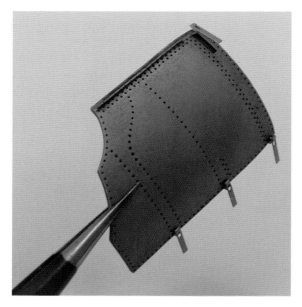

Small etched brass cowling latches are fitted prior to fixing the cowlings in place.

BELOW: *The cowlings are now in place. The cable stays have been attached to the cowlings, and some extra soft wire, leading to the engine accessories, has been added. The cable stays on the cowlings are supplied on the engine etched brass sheet. These were very easily damaged, so the end fittings were used with EZ line, a fine stretchable thread that ensures the cable stays taut.*

FINAL ASSEMBLY AND CONCLUSION

The remaining parts to be fitted, all from the plastic kit, were the aerials on the underside, a retractable footstep and the canopy. The propeller assembly, flaps and fan disc were the last parts to be fitted.

It is possible to build a model giving a similar level of detail by using the standard Revell kit and scratch building the detail. However, not every modeller has the skills required for scratch building, and the products used on this example gave a far greater in-depth detail than even many a seasoned scratch builder can. Patience is the most important attribute needed in getting the most out of these large detail sets. A modeller with some experience should be able to use them and achieve a good standard of finish. Some builders will want even more detail than that portrayed here. The beauty of doing this kind of detail work is that you can take it as far as your skills allow.

The finished project sitting on one of Coastal Kit's bases.

A closer view of the starboard side engine bay area.

Scale Conversion Chart

The table shown below covers all the regular aircraft and helicopter scales and may help you to carry out conversions for scratch building, or to carry out a whole kit scale conversion.

The sample shown is to convert 1/72 scale to 1/32 scale: the answer is you must multiply by 2.250.

If you wish to go from 1/32 scale to 1/72 you will need to divide by 0.444.

Scale Conversion Table Matrix

	A	B	C	D	E	F	G
	Scale	24	32	35	48	72	144
1							
2	24	1.000	0.750	0.686	0.500	0.333	0.167
3	32	1.333	1.000	0.914	0.667	0.444	0.222
4	35	1.458	1.094	1.000	0.729	0.486	0.243
5	48	2.000	1.500	1.371	1.000	0.667	0.333
6	72	3.000	2.250	2.057	1.500	1.000	0.500
7	144	6.000	4.500	4.114	3.000	2.000	1.000

Choose Scale from column A (From)
Choose Scale from Row 1 (To)
Multiply by the factor in the intersecting cell

Glossary

3D Three dimensions.

anneal Brass which is heated up until it glows red and then cooled down or quenched in water.

AOA Angle of attack.

CAD Computer-aided design.

capillary action The ability of fluids to flow into narrow spaces even against gravity.

chain drilling Drilling a series of holes where a straight cut is required, but there is no access for a saw.

cowling Aircraft engine cover.

dihedral The upward angle of aircraft wings.

doubler plate An additional plate attached to the wing or fuselage to strengthen or to repair damage.

durometer Resistance to indentation in silicon rubber.

firewall Usually a stainless-steel bulkhead between the engine bay and the cockpit.

fret The framework of a sheet of etched brass components.

magnetos Distributors for all the spark-plug leads.

nacelle the streamlined casing housing the aircraft engine and sometimes undercarriage.

oil canning Aircraft skins look as if they are ballooned out and the rivet runs are slightly recessed.

pitot tube Airspeed measuring device protruding from aircraft wings or fuselage.

pounce wheel Traditional sign writers' or artists' tools, these are wheels held in a fork and handle, with evenly spaced teeth.

riffler Set of specially shaped files.

sprue The framework to which plastic model parts are attached.

Useful Contacts

Airbrush Company Ltd
Airbrushing equipment and paints.
The Airbrush Company Ltd
79 Marlborough Road (East)
Lancing Business Park
Lancing, West Sussex BN15 8UF
Tel. +44 (0) 1903 767800
www.airbrushes.com sales@airbrushes.com

airscale
Instrument panels, instrument and placard decals.
https://airscale.co.uk

Aires/Quickboost
Cast resin detail sets.
www.aires.cz & www.quickboost.net info@aires.cz
Aires, spol. s.r.o.
Horanska cesta 703
434 01 Most
Czech Republic

Army painter
A wide range of specialist model paint brushes and acrylic paint.
www.thearmypainter.com contact@thearmy-painter.com

CMK
Cast resin detail sets.
https://cmkkits.com office@specialhobby.eu

Coastal Kits
Display bases.
www.coastalkits.co.uk contact@coastalkits.co.uk

Eduard Models
Eduard – Model Accessories.spol.s.r.o
Mirova 170
435 21 Obrnice
Czech Republic
IC: 44564325 DIC CZ44564325
https://www.eduard.com support@eduard.com

Expo Drills & Tools
Unit 6
The Salterns
Tenby
SA70 7NJ
https://www.expotools.com info@expotools.com

Hannants Model Kits and Accessories
H. G. Hannant Ltd
Unit 2 Hurricane Trading Estate
Grahame Park Way
Colingdale
London NW9 5QW
Tel 0208 205 6697
www.hannants.co.uk sales@hannants.co.uk

HGW Models
Decal rivet sets.
https://hgwmodels.cz info@hgwmodels.cz

Master-Model
Turned brass gun barrels and accessories.
www.master-model.pl info@master-model.pl

Model Motorcars Ltd
Metal rivets, nuts and bolts and other hardware.
www.modelmotorcars.com

Modelkasten
Precision Photofabrication Developers Ltd
(PPD Ltd)
Photo etch production.
www.ppdltd.com enquiries@ppdltd.com

Neomega-Resin
High quality resin accessories.
Studio G008
The Atkins Building
Lower Bond Street
Hinckley LE10 1QU
www.neomega-resin.com sales@neomega-resin.
com

Premier Brush Co.
Art and craft paint brushes.
www.premierbrush.co.uk info@premierbrush.
co.uk
Premier Brush Limited
Little Chantersluer
Smalls Hill Road
Norwood Hill, Horley
Surrey RH6 0HR

Proper Plane
Laminated wood propellers and hollow metal
exhausts.
www.properplane.com

R. B. Productions
7 The Mall
Main Street
Leixlip, Co Kildare
W23 X725
IRELAND
https://www.radubstore.com

Scalewarship Ltd
Photo etch drawing and paint mask service.
5 Beechwood Avenue
New Milton
Hampshire BH25 5NB
Tel 01425 618640
Mobile 07855 941117
www.scalewarship.com Johnw@scalewarship.
com

Small Stuff Models
Highly detailed model aircraft engines.
www.smallstuffmodels.com info@smallstuffmod-
els.com

Reference List

BOOKS AND OTHER PUBLICATIONS

Carpenter, Robin *Airbrushing Scale Model Aircraft*.

Caruana, Richard (edited by Alan Hall) *Warpaint Special No.3 de Havilland Mosquito*.

Craighead, Ian *Haynes Manual Rolls-Royce Merlin Engine*.

Eagle Editions Ltd *Eaglecals EC166 Instruction Sheet*.

Falconer, Jonathan and Rivas, Brian *Haynes Manual de Havilland Mosquito*.

Horne and Hauseman *AP3D Printing for Dummies (2nd Edition)*.

Ovcacik, Michael and Susa, Karel *4+ Publication Westland Wessex*.

Redwood, Schoffer and Garret *The 3D Printing Handbook, Technologies, Design and Applications*.

Stafrace, Charles *Warpaint Series No.65 Westland Wessex*.

Thirsk, Ian *de Havilland Mosquito, An Illustrated history Volume 2*.

Wallach, Kloski and Kloski *Getting Started with 3D Printing*.

Westland Wessex Maintenance Manual *AP101C—0105-1A*.

WEBSITES

http://www.britmodeller.com/forums/index.php?/forum/341-rotary-wing-aircraft-walkarounds/

COMPUTER PROGRAMS

Fusion 360 by Autodesk.

Rhino: Robert McNeel & Associates.

SolidWorks: Dassault Systemes@.

SketchUp: @Last Software.

Index

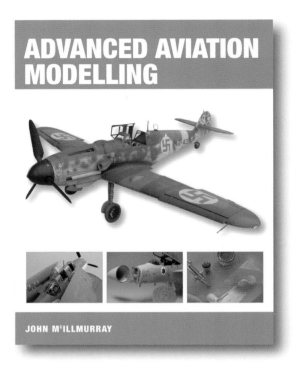

ADVANCED AVIATION MODELLING

JOHN McILLMURRAY

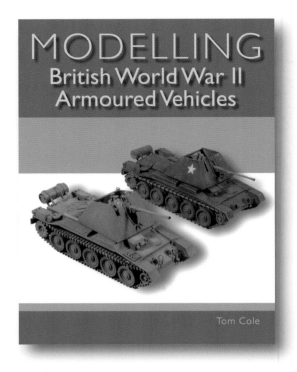

MODELLING British World War II Armoured Vehicles

Tom Cole

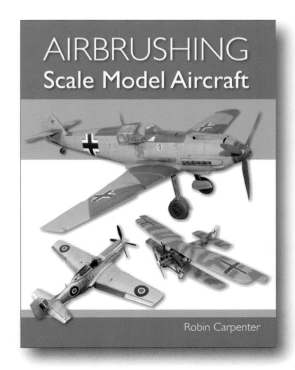

AIRBRUSHING Scale Model Aircraft

Robin Carpenter

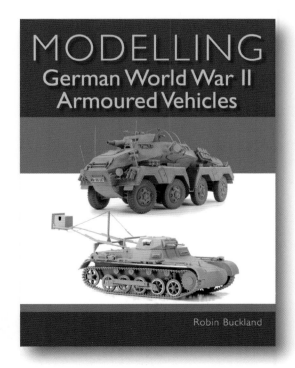

MODELLING German World War II Armoured Vehicles

Robin Buckland